Growing Up on the Farm

Clydeane Gorham

Please direct all correspondence and book orders to:

Robert Wall
270 Muscovy Trail
Sumter, S.C. 29150
Phone: 803-469-4014

ISBN: 0-9769229-9-1

Published by:

www.BarbaraMartin.net
YOU SHOULD WRITE A BOOK

Beaufort, S.C.
843-263-5248
E-mail: barbara@barbaramartin.net

Photos supplied by the author
Cover photo: the author in Memphis, 1943
Cover design by Barbara Martin

Synopsis

Growing Up on the Farm is a delightful autobiography of a young girl's life growing up on a Kentucky farm in the midst of the Great Depression. Beginning when she is about eight years old in 1930, it covers a multitude of almost forgotten tidbits of what life was like years ago on the farm. It will bring back pleasant memories for all those who had similar experiences on a farm and enlighten those who didn't with stories from the "low-tech" world of yesteryear seen through a child's eyes.

Bygone days are brought to life again through her charming memories of the one-room school, plowing with a horse, riding a horse to school, Model T Fords, eavesdropping on a party line, chopping cotton, and the Saturday night bath, to name a few.

The book describes how these self-reliant and self-sufficient Americans provided for themselves, in a time when people had little money, by growing and preserving their own food and making their own clothes, their own soap, and their own butter.

To illustrate the narrative, numerous photos—some more than a hundred years old—are included.

Readers interested in history and genealogy will enjoy this book enormously. Young people involved in the "back to the land" movement will gain valuable information about farming, food storage, and other practical skills.

Despite hardships and grueling sunup-to-sundown workdays, the author remembers a life filled with happiness and optimism.

Growing Up on the Farm is a joy to read and is suitable for all age groups.

Growing Up on the Farm

Introduction

My name is Clydeane Gorham. I was born on December 28, 1921, in Bardwell, Carlisle County, Kentucky. The date is August 12, 1995. I am seventy-three years old, in good health and fair memory. I have just talked by phone to my brother, Joe R. Gorham, and he said that I needed to write down my memories of what life was like growing up in Kentucky during the Depression on our farm. First let me state that I am not a writer. I am a very poor speller and have no plan as to how to go about getting this down so anyone would read it, much less be interested. I shall start off by setting down a few things that come to mind, and later these ramblings can be edited and assembled in some kind of order that may be of help to those who are doing genealogy research on our family.

Me
1922

Mama, Mora Underwood Gorham, holding me
1922

Starting School

I have no records as to when we (Dad, Mom, Betty and I) moved from Port Arthur, Texas, back to Carlisle County, Kentucky, on my grandfather's farm. The best I can figure, it must have been sometime in 1930. My sister, Betty, was born on Christmas Day 1928, and I distinctly remember her birthday when she was one year old and we were living in Texas.

Also, when I went to kindergarten in DeQueen School in Port Arthur, I was six years old three days before the end of the year 1927. Therefore, I was able to start kindergarten at age five. That would make me start the first grade

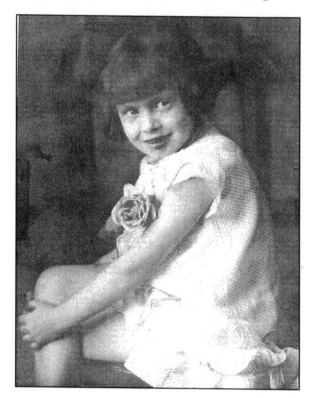

Me in Texas

1927

at six, starting the second grade at seven, and starting the third grade at eight in 1930.

I remember my disappointment when we found out that the "One Room School" (with only one teacher for all grades) only taught first, second, third, fifth and seventh grades one year, then first, second, fourth, sixth and eighth grades the next year. Since I only had "low third," the first half of the third grade, in Texas my parents thought

Dad. Albert Ray Gorham
About 1931

I would be unable to keep up if I skipped to the fifth, so they made me take the third grade again. This was very devastating to me since I was a top student in a very progressive Texas city school having to transfer to a rural Kentucky one-room school. Needless to say, I was bored with my third-grade class and spent most of my time at school listening to the upper classes recite, which in turn was old material when I was passed to that class. Therefore, I was bored again and, consequently, not a very good student.

Playing the Piano

Life on the farm was very busy. There were so many chores for an eight-year-old to do, and I had to walk a mile to and from school each day.

My piano teacher Ruth Gorham

At age nine, I came home from school one day and found a large upright piano in our living room. Dad had ordered it delivered from Paducah. It must have cost fifty dollars. I then started walking almost a mile once a week to take piano lessons from my second cousin, Ruth Gorham.

After dinner, Mom would say, "Clydeane, can you do the supper dishes or do you have to practice?" Of all the chores I was told to do, washing supper dishes was the only one I really hated. I guess it was no surprise to anyone that I chose to practice. Smart woman that Mom was, she always made the dish washing job last until she heard me practice all of my lesson and several hymns extra.

By the time I completed my third music book, Ruth told Dad that she could no longer teach me because I played hymns better than she did. So Dad arranged for me to take piano from the Bardwell School music teacher at her home every Saturday for fifty cents a lesson. Rain or shine, I went to town with Dad in the wagon and walked several blocks up the hill to take my music lesson.

After I acted as substitute pianist for several months, the church elected me as the church pianist when I was about twelve. Dad was proud that his daughter was the church pianist and saw to it that I never missed a service.

During Daily Vacation Bible School, he let me ride our old mare to and from church. We had a volunteer choir led by Mr. Arthur Bishop who taught me a bunch of signals from him as when to stop, start, slow down, and a few others. When given the opportunity of picking the songs for the day, I always picked hymns that had strong bass or alto leads because we had Mr. Rhonie Terry and Mrs. Thelma Wilson, who had outstanding voices. They kept electing me as the church pianist until I went away to Murray State College at age nineteen.

Paw

My grandfather, Elisha Milton Gorham, whom I called Paw, had lived alone so many years, he was delighted to have us back on the farm, and I was the apple of his eye. I remember our milch cows spent the day in a pasture on the back side of the farm and did not know (or want to know) when dusk was approaching and it time to come to the barn to be fed corn and milked. So Paw, our big farm dog, Popeye, and I would go find the cows in the back field and drive them up to the barn.

Paw, Elisha Milton Gorham
About 1920

Cows are orderly creatures and would follow the lead cow, single file along the same path through the field to the barn until they would have a nice hard path worn through the knee-high grass and weeds.

Growing girl that I was and having long legs, I would run ahead along the path and frequently would run up on a long black snake stretched out across the path, sunning itself. Coming up on him so fast before I saw him, I would leap over and, when safely away, would call out, "Snake! Snake!"

Paw would calmly walk up and put his left foot right behind the snake's head, holding it down while slowly (it seemed) taking out and opening his pocketknife. Then he would bend down and, with one stroke, cut the snake's head off. All this time the rear end of the snake was busy coiling itself around Paw's leg.

I don't have to tell you that to an eight-year-old city girl, Elisha Milton Gorham was the bravest man on earth. I always smiled in appreciation when I noticed that, while relaxing, he would be honing his knife blade on the leather side of his shoe.

Next page, top:
Mom and Dad
on their wedding day
1920

Next page, bottom:
Paw (center) with his brothers
Byron (left) and James
About 1920

9

Right:
Dad in World War I

Below:
Mom at about fifteen years old
About 1915

Popeye

Paw killed a few snakes in this manner, but Popeye was our number one snake killer. Popeye was supposed to be our stock dog but I don't remember him being particularly good at herding livestock. However, he was especially adept at killing snakes.

He was a large mongrel dog and was mainly white except for a large brown spot around his left eye. He would run ahead of me and investigate everything before I could get to it. I know now that he was probably checking everything out to make sure it was okay and safe for me.

Whenever he found a snake he would pick it up by the midsection and flail it to death before it had a chance to strike him. Similar to the way a dog can shake off after getting wet, he would shake the snake from side to side so violently that the snake would be flailed to pieces. Usually the head would fly off as well as some other pieces, but at the least, its back would be broken in many places.

Popeye really loved me and I loved him. He looked out for me and, consequently, dogs and horses have always been my favorite animals. Both are so loving and faithful.

Milking the Cows

After driving the cows up to the barn and getting them into their respective stalls, Paw would let me help feed them and, while they were eating, he would milk them. At times, some of the cows would have calves, which were kept in the adjacent stalls. The mother cow, knowing her baby was pawing the earth floor to get to her, would "hold up" about half of her milk, so when Paw had milked his half, he would call out to me to let the calf in. When I unbolted the door, the young critter would come charging in and almost knock the mother cow over grabbing for the milk. Paw and I would get a good laugh about how the mother cows didn't seem to mind how rough their babies were getting their milk, but as the calves grew larger and could butt harder trying to get their mother to give down more milk, some cows would give them a swift kick. When Paw noticed this, he would say it was time to wean the calf, and it would be put out into a separate pasture to graze for its livelihood.

All of this was of such interest to me that I began to pester Paw to teach me to milk the cows. I think he thought I was too young, but he hardly ever said no to me, so I was taught to milk and was so good at it that it became one of my chores.

For several years, during the summer after we came in from working in the field, I would milk two cows each night while Paw milked two or sometimes three. However, he never let me milk a cow that had a nursing calf unless it was an emergency and then he cautioned me to get out of the stall before the calf was let in. Also, during the school term, I was never asked to milk in the morning time because the school bus came early.

I am not complaining about all the chores and other work from before sunup until after sunset because I knew that we all worked hard. I really didn't mind, for after all Paw was there to help me if there was heavy work to be done, and he had all the patience in the world. He listened to my incessant talking, never saying a word unless I asked a question or he needed to explain something to me.

My younger brother, Joe, was taught to milk the cows at an early age. Whenever he had to milk a cow that had a calf that needed to be weaned, he would use the milking stool to drive away the calf after the cow had let down her remaining milk. The calves were very determined to get the milk and were not receptive to subtle hints that they were no longer welcome to it.

After the mother cow would let down her remaining milk, Joe would bash the calf in the head with the milking stool until the calf was driven away. Quite often this required a dozen or more strong whacks from the stool before the calf would give up.

Once, while milking, Joe asked our sister, Betty, to go find a stick or something to drive away the calf. When Betty returned she held up a tiny twig between her two fingers and asked, "Do you think this is going to hurt him?" Joe then began laughing so hard that he fell backwards off the milking stool.

The Ol' Mare

Another important part of my farm life was a mare horse that we simply called "the Ol' Mare." She was a large buggy horse bay with a blaze face. I don't know how old she was when we moved back to the farm, but she wasn't young, and after serving her time pulling a buggy, she was the farm's brood mare. She had two beautiful bay mules (matched pair) and a dark gray mule called Jack, maybe more.

Shortly after I got accustomed to living on the farm and became buddies with my grandfather, he got out Dad's old army-type saddle and saddled up the Ol' Mare and helped me up. I'll never understand it because I was from the city and had never been on a horse, and the Ol' Mare was a smart old girl with a whole bag of tricks she used to bluff and scare people off from riding her. Yet she let me ride her, and if she ever pulled a trick to scare me off, I was too dumb to know it.

Soon I was riding all over that end of the county and loving it. I rode more than two miles to church when they had Daily Vacation Bible School because my parents were too busy to take me. Also, I rode three miles to visit a cousin and about four miles to visit my Aunt Muriel. The Ol' Mare always seemed anxious to get home, so I let her go as fast as she wanted, and I was told that one of the old ladies along the road was heard to say over the "party line" telephone, "I just saw that long-legged Clydeane racing by on her horse so fast her hair was standing straight out in back." It was true; she really could go fast. In fact, I had a few friends who had a quarter horse or pinto pony, but my Ol' Mare could pass them like they were standing still.

I was never told what gait she used, but in later years I have come to believe that she did a "single foot" or "rack" for while going fast, she rode really easy, but when she slowed to a trot, you were in for a bumpy ride.

A War of Wits

As a young man Dad had taught school. Then after serving in World War I, he learned typing and telegraphy and moved with Mom and me to Port Arthur, Texas. I must have been around three years old for I remember very little of our early days in Texas. He worked as the ship's clerk and radio operator for the Gulf Refining Company on an oil tanker for all the years before returning to Kentucky during the Great Depression. Don't let it be said that he didn't work hard as a farmer, but he didn't like it. So he had the attitude, "When I work, everybody works!"

Each spring, we all turned out to work on the day we were to plant the garden. Paw studied *The Farmer's Almanac* and knew when it was the right time. We had about a six-acre fenced garden, and Dad would hitch the mule team to the large turning plow to "break it up." Then after using a smaller plow to throw up the dirt into ridges or rows, he would use a light harrow to knock off the top of the rows. This made a nice flat place to plant the seeds or set out plants, etc.

I had a large part in the planting because I could bend over easily to drop seed potatoes, cabbage plants, and other seeds, etc.

After a few weeks of sun, rain and plant growth, the weeds would be gaining on us, so Dad took a (yet smaller) cultivating plow or "double shovel" to plow between the rows, thus knocking out the weeds. This "middle buster" was a single horse plow, so Dad hitched up the Ol' Mare to it and advanced to the garden to "bust weeds" for the first time since returning to the farm. Friends, right here is where the "war of wits" began. The Ol' Mare, being the smart old girl that she was, took off right down the top of the row with the cute young peas and carrots going every which way, just like the weeds were supposed to do. No manner of yelling and yanking on the reins that Dad could do would get her off the top of the row, and what she didn't plow up, she stomped on.

Dad was furious, so at the end of the row, Paw stopped and turned the Ol' Mare and plow around and said, "I'll plow the next row."

Then Paw marched over, in front of the mare so she could see that he went to the side of the garden where there was a peach tree and, with his wonderful pocketknife, cut a long, slim switch.

I have often wondered if a horse's eyes worked independently of each other for they can see everything that happens on either side and even behind them. That is why all our bridles had "blinders" on them so the horse would have to turn its head to see to the side.

You can bet Ol' Mare was watching Paw as he stripped the leaves off the long, keen switch. Then he came back, picked up the reins, and said, "You just have to let her know who is boss." He yelled, "Gee-up" and gave her a smart rap on the rump with the switch. She took off right down the middle between the rows and never once stepped on a vegetable.

Going to Town

Our farm was five miles west of Bardwell, Kentucky, and that entire five miles was dirt road, up and down hills and crooked around the property line of all the farms west of Bardwell.

During the winter the dirt road would become deep ruts of mud that would not dry up from one rain to another. Although my grandfather owned a Model T Ford, after the roads got muddy we had to go to town (Bardwell) each Saturday in our wagon. The "matched mule team" was very slow, so Dad decided to use one of the mules and the Ol' Mare to pull the wagon, and it was quite a bit faster.

The Ol' Mare, being the matriarch of the horses, was accustomed to leading so she walked half a head in front of the mule. Therefore, she just about wore herself out pulling most of the wagon load. So before starting the five-mile trip home, Dad shortened the mule's trace chains by tying a knot or two in them, just enough so the Ol' Mare could still walk ahead, yet the mule pulled his share (or maybe more) of the load.

Unless the weather was too bad, we all went to town every Saturday. Dad and Mom sat on the wagon's spring seat, and my little sister, Betty, sat between them, but I had to sit on a plank that was put across the wagon bed. Five miles to and from town sitting on a hard plank riding on a rough dirt road was a bit harder on my pride than my rear end since we would see other families going to town. They had three or four spring seats on their wagon, enough to seat their whole family in comfort. Of course, those families did not own a car so they fitted their wagon to be comfortable all year. Anyway, I remember being jealous and making myself a promise: "When I get grown and rich, I will have a wagon with two spring seats."

I really loved the Ol' Mare because we were such good buddies. When I was pretty small and the weather would turn bad while I was in school, Dad would ride her to come pick me up. Then I would ride behind him and hold on to his belt while we went home.

When I got bigger I rode her to school myself on days when snow was on the ground or after a big rain. On days like this the other kids would do the same thing, and you would see several horses tied to the fence outside the schoolhouse. The Ol' Mare didn't like this because she was afraid that some of the other horses might not be friendly toward me, so she would always position herself between me and the other horses. She really looked out for me.

On cold and snowy days, I would ride the Ol' Mare with a blanket draped over us. Dad had cut a hole in the blanket that was big enough for me to put it over my head and pull it down to my waist. I would then spread it out over the horse and we would keep each other warm.

In later years, some of our distant cousins who were very poor came and borrowed her from Paw to do some plowing. They hitched her with two mules to make the third in a triple tree. Quite often horses don't get along too well with mules and, given the opportunity, they will go in front of the mules. So naturally the mules would hang back and let her do most of the work. Since she turned out to be such a willing worker, our cousins allowed this to happen, and they ended up working her to death.

I really cried over the death of the Ol' Mare because I loved her so much.

Paw's Railroad Watch

Paw did not like to go to town every Saturday, but he went every five or six weeks in order to set his watch. He owned two pocket watches. One was a dollar watch with a plaited leather watch fob that he wore every day in his overall bib pocket. This fob was a plaited leather cord attached to the watch and your clothing to make sure you didn't drop the watch.

However, his pride and joy was his "railroad watch," which had a nice gold chain and fob. When he spoke of this watch, he always said, "my twenty-three jewel railroad watch," and he kept all the house clocks and watches set to this twenty-three jewel railroad watch. He would go to town every so often just to verify his watch against the railroad station clock and

Paw sporting his watch fob and chain
About 1891

would proudly tell you his watch was off only a second or two in several months.

I was always glad when Paw went into town because he brought home a quarter's worth of candy, which was a large sack, and Mama always had to watch to keep me from eating too much in one day and making myself sick. Then Paw would always buy himself a very large stick of peppermint candy that he squirreled away in his private trunk and, at his bedtime each night, he would chip off a bite to hold in his mouth after going to bed. I often wondered if the fact that he had run out of peppermint wasn't the deciding factor in his trip to town rather than setting his perfect watch.

Paw also had a very nice eight-day mantle clock that he wound up every Sunday and set by his twenty-three jewel watch. The clock had a nice porcelain face, and the glass door had a gold filigree design that set off the ornamental pendulum. I liked that clock, and the family used to laugh and tell me that, as a very young child, I would stand in front of the clock and sway back and forth in time with the swinging of the pendulum. Paw told me once that he gave fifty cents for the clock, which was hard for me to believe, but during the Depression, a grown man would work all day for fifty cents.

When I started dating I learned to hate that clock because it told the hour by striking about as loudly as England's Big Ben. At breakfast the morning following my date, Dad or Paw would ask me from across the table, "What time did you get in last night?" and I didn't dare lie about it because I knew they knew what time I had gotten in.

Dad's Whippet

Dad was fed up with the Model T Ford because it was a fair weather car. When it rained you had to get out and put up the side curtains—*if* you brought them with you. The "T" didn't have a trunk, so the curtains were usually left in the garage. One could really get soaked by the time he got the leather curtains up, and it was hard to see out as they had little isinglass windows stitched somewhere in the curtain—not necessarily at a place and height where one could look out. So one day he came home driving a new car, a Whippet. It was a luxury car with glass windows that rolled up and down. The seats had beautiful upholstery and a little rosebud vase on each side by the back door. Best of all, a real status symbol, it had a huge ornament on the motor meter, which is what everyone called the little thermometer on the radiator cap that was supposed to tell you if the water in the radiator got too hot. I don't know what year this was, but I am guessing it was 1932 or 1933.

Now, the roads that had bad mud holes and ruts in the winter were not much better in the summer for they had deep dust ruts. In fact, one didn't have to worry about having a head-on collision when the narrow road had a ninety-degree turn, for one was well aware that someone was approaching by the cloud of dust visible long before you got to the turn.

Dad's Whippet, which would have been right at home on the streets of Chicago (during the Prohibition era), was not practical for dirt roads. However, he was very proud to drive it to church and town and talk about how much automobiles had advanced with gear shift, clutch, self-starter, mechanical windshield wipers, etc.

Several weeks passed and Dad had not shown Mom how to drive the Whippet.

Mom was a good driver of the T. With my help, she would set the spark lever and go around to the front and turn the crank until the engine started. Then she would yell for me to "give it the gas," and I would pull the gas lever down to a certain mark, which would keep it going until she could run around and get in and start manipulating the three foot pedals. One pedal made it go, one made it back up, and I don't know what the other one was for.

Mom was really put out with Dad's excuses for not teaching her to drive the Whippet, so she asked my Aunt Muriel, who had a Dodge with a gear shift, to teach her how to drive it. Aunt Muriel drew her a diagram of the shift pattern (in the shape of an H) marking the low, second, high and reverse positions. While everyone was in the field or somewhere, Mom would slip down to the barn where the car was garaged behind a door that slid on a track. After going into the garage, she would slide the door to a closed position so no one would notice she was there practicing the shift pattern.

I don't know how long she had been doing this, but one afternoon I was sitting on the front porch wondering where everyone had gone when I heard a loud "bam-bam" noise coming from the barn. I jumped up and started running down to the barn, and there was Mom in the Whippet backing out of the garage without sliding the door open, so it just went up like it was hinged, and the car was halfway out from under it before she got it stopped. Surprisingly, she was quite calm and told me that she had practiced shifting until she felt that she knew it, so she started the engine. Since she hadn't depressed the clutch, she was fortunate that the car was in reverse when she started it. Otherwise, it would have gone under a hay frame that was hung in the other end of the garage, and she probably would have been decapitated.

Picture this: The Whippet was half out of the garage with the bottom of the large wooden sliding garage door on top of it, and I was having an anxiety fit thinking what Dad would do when he came in from the field and saw it. I have never been prouder of Mom's control under pressure as she said, "I'll finish backing the car out and, when the door falls down, you slide it open, and I'll drive the car back in the garage." Then she did. No one but the two of us would have ever known about the incident except for the fact that when she backed out from under the door, it swung down off the top of the car, missed the hood, but clipped off the ornament on the motor meter as clean as a whistle. I don't know if Dad was disenchanted with the Whippet because the status symbol was gone or if it was because of the bad roads, but soon he got rid of the Whippet and got us a Model A Ford.

Sunday Dessert

In 1933, Franklin D. Roosevelt became president, and soon after he put into effect several programs, one being the Square Deal or WPA (Works Progress Administration) or something that gave us a gravel highway from Bardwell to Columbus, Kentucky. It was great—no more steep hills or sharp curves and corners around the farmers' property lines. In fact, it came right across our farm and almost got our barn. The good part is that we no longer had to go to town in the wagon when the weather got bad. It was too bad that Dad had gotten rid of his Whippet because he had enjoyed it so much when the roads permitted him to drive it.

Since it didn't take us long to go to and from town in the Model A on the good highway, Dad started to bring us a one hundred pound block of ice home on our Saturday trip to town. We didn't have an icebox, so Dad would drive the Model A up to the house and into the side yard we called the wood lot and put the ice block in a number two washtub. We loved it, for we could have iced tea or lemonade for Sunday dinner, and we usually made ice cream late on Sunday afternoon with fresh peaches, strawberries or raspberries from our garden. We would all help unload the car and then run in the house to change into our work clothes to do our evening chores, etc., and sometimes Dad would get busy and forget to back the car down to the garage. I don't know how long it took him to figure out who was backing the car down and putting it in the garage because I was only about thirteen at that time. However, they were letting me drive anywhere I wanted to go by age fourteen. A driver's license was not a requirement in our county in 1935.

The Orchard's Bounty

When we moved back to the farm, our orchard was badly in need of pruning. Paw was unable to climb the trees due to a back injury several years before, so Dad got a young man to come over and help him prune.

The orchard was at least ten acres, maybe more. There were a couple rows of early apples, three or four rows of apples that ripened later, and two rows of late apples.

At the end of the rows close to the house were peach and pear trees, so Dad and the young man worked hard sawing off large limbs, and Paw hitched a mule to the limbs and dragged them off to a field to be burned.

Mom was afraid they had cut them back so severely that they would die, but within a year or two we had so many apples that Mom canned so many Mason jars of applesauce, peaches and pears that she filled our root cellar and Dad had to dig a bigger one. She also fixed dried apples that she used to make fried pies that I loved to take in my school lunch box. In fact, Dad would gather enough apples to fill a couple of washtubs we had on the back porch before he went out in the field to plow or something. Then Paw and I would sit in cane bottom chairs and peel apples for Mom to can until my fingers would shrivel up from taking them out of the water. The late apples were McIntosh, and we gathered and put them in hampers in the root cellar, so we had fresh apples to eat almost all winter. Mom made apple jelly, peach and pear preserves as well as canned fruit for apple and peach cobbler pies.

Mom's work didn't stop there. We had a huge garden,

and she canned vegetables, made kraut, and since we had early and late strawberry patches and a grape arbor, she made strawberry preserves and grape jelly. No wonder that, all summer, we carried a one hundred pound sack of sugar home from town every week.

No one in our family ever believed in wasting anything, so Dad went somewhere and bought an apple cider mill and, when he thought Mom had filled the root cellar enough, he would call a halt to that and we would make cider out the rest of the apples. It wasn't as much work, for we would shake the trees, pick up the apples and pour them in a couple of tubs of water for a little while. We would then dip them out with a bucket and pour them into the mill and it would grind up apple, peal, seeds, worms and all. We took turns turning the crank, and the juice would come out into buckets. Dad would have planned ahead for this and asked the owner of the town soda fountain to save him the barrel when all the coke syrup had been used up. I don't know what Dad paid for the barrel, but it couldn't have been much for we had very little money. I do know that the wooden barrel had absorbed enough coke syrup that it flavored the cider, and that made a good drink.

My School Lunch

Mom, Dad and Paw worked so hard from before sunup until well after sundown, and of course they kept me busy too, but I never realized that some of our relatives and neighbors thought of us as being well off until, one day while at school, a little girl a couple of years younger than I was came up to me at lunchtime and said, "When you are finished with your apple, can I have the core?"

Mom always fixed me a good lunch. Whatever we had for breakfast she saved enough for my lunch—some days biscuit and ham and other days biscuit and sausage and sometimes chicken. Whatever dessert was left from Sunday dinner went into my lunch, such as pie or cake, and when that ran out she would make fried apple pie, which was my favorite.

When our early apple trees started having ripe apples, she would always put one of those in too. It depended on what the dessert was whether or not I ate the apple. I would take a bite or two to take the sweet taste out of my mouth and throw it away. I suppose the girl had watched me do this and thought it such a waste since they didn't have any apples. When she asked for my core, I had taken a bite out of the apple, but when I saw the pleading look on her face, I said, "Sure," and handed it to her.

After that, I guess Mom wondered why I asked for two apples in my lunch each day.

Gathering Nuts

The first fall that we were back in Kentucky, Mom gave me a bucket and she took two and we went down to the area that we did not cultivate because it was wooded. Dad and Paw cut our firewood from there. It also had a nice natural spring that flowed good water all year long. They would let the cows that had nursing calves run in this area because they would not put them with the other cows that were being milked until the calf was sold for veal. In the fall, it was beautiful, and Mom took me to help her pick up nuts because she said that on a winter evening while sitting around the fire we could eat chestnuts, hickory nuts and black walnuts.

I learned to stomp the chestnut burrs with the heel of my shoe and grab the three or four chestnuts out without the burr sticking in my fingers. The black walnuts had to be stomped out too, but instead of sticking your fingers, their hulls had a black dye that, once you got it on your hands, was almost impossible to get off.

The scaly bark hickory nuts were easier to pick out of their hulls because they were mostly open when the nuts fell. The only problem was that the hogs and other animals knew they were easy, so they tried to beat us to them.

That winter I really enjoyed eating these nuts while baking my shins by the wood-burning circulating heater. Therefore, the next fall Mom learned where more trees were and, starting earlier with me now an experienced nut gatherer, we soon picked up our winter supply. However, Mom and I kept on picking up chestnuts and got a long cotton sack filled. Mom had Dad ship them for sale to a place in St. Louis, and the company sent her a check for nine dollars. Mom and I sat down with a Sears catalog and ordered enough material for Mom to make all the winter and spring clothes for my little sister and me. Sears had some very pretty cloth for as little as nine cents a yard.

Years later, I was sorry to learn that most of our chestnut trees died when the blight went through the country for they were a helping hand for us during the Depression.

The Chickens

Early each spring, Dad would disk up the orchard ground and sew it in oats, barley or wheat to keep it from growing up in weeds. It also served as a feeding place for the mother hens to take their flocks of little chicks. The mother hen could teach her babies to scratch up worms and other bugs because the ground had been worked up and was soft. As the grain started to grow, it was a perfect place for the little chicks to hide from hawks. Some folks say that chickens are the dumbest creatures on the farm, but I have watched a hen with about three dozen chicks scratch up a bug and make a certain call to her chicks. Then they would all rush in to see what she had found and fight over which one would get it. Another time, if she saw a hawk flying around, she would call out again and they would all scurry into the grain plants to hide, and you could not see a one. Every now and then a hawk would see a chick that was slow to hide and the hawk would make a dive after the chick. This wonderful mother hen would go into action and attack the hawk with all her feathers standing out and wings spread, looking twice her regular size, and either scare or fight off the hawk. I guess the hawk learned a lesson the day he was flogged by a mother hen.

Mom always had a flock of about one hundred chickens, mostly White Rock or Rhode Island Red because that breed made larger, plumper and whiter meat fryers. She cooked two each Sunday for dinner all spring, summer and fall. These hens were good egg producers, too.

One of my chores was to feed the chickens about the

same time every day so the chickens got in the habit of coming up from the orchard or field before dark. This kept them safe from foxes, possums and other chicken thieves. I had to go down to the barn corncrib and shell (we had a hand-turned sheller) about three quarters of a bucket of corn. I was never able to shuck much corn because my wrists were not strong enough, so Paw always had a pile of shucked corn near the sheller for me. I also shelled enough corn to run through the hand-turned grinder to feed the baby chicks when their mother brought them up to the chicken yard to be closed into their coops for the night.

These coops were little houses (much like a doghouse) made out of wood with a roof to keep out the rain. They also had a plank floor so a rat or something could not dig under at night to steal a chick.

Early in the spring all the hens started laying more eggs, and the henhouse fairly rocked with the sound of the hens doing their cackling after laying their daily egg. In the fall and wintertime, Mom asked me to gather the eggs late each afternoon, but in the spring, Mom did it because she was watching the hens for signs that they wanted to "set." When she noticed a particular hen staying on the nest after laying her egg, and when she came out of the henhouse to eat the corn I threw out in late afternoon making a little clucking sound like she was calling chicks, Mom knew she was about to start "setting on her eggs to make babies." Mom would wait until she had three hens that wanted to set. Then she would put about fifteen eggs under each of them on the same day. In three weeks, the three hens' eggs would start to "pip." Then, within two or three days, all the eggs would be hatched out. It didn't seem fair to me, but Mom would gather all the chicks and put them in a coop with one mother hen. Then she would re-set the other two hens and probably another one that was willing.

If anyone believes that hens are dumb, ask them to explain how a setting hen knows to turn each of her eggs every day to make sure all the eggs will hatch. Also, how does the hen that mothers three dozen chicks keep up with all those babies and teach them to scratch for food and come up to the chicken yard at dusk and go into their assigned coop for the night? Of course, those who believe that chickens are so dumb surely only have had experience around chickens that were obtained from hatcheries.

After I grew up and left for school, Mom started getting one or two hundred chicks hatched in hatcheries. These chicks were raised in a wire pen and never had a mother hen to take them to the orchard and teach them to hide from a hawk or scratch for food.

One thing I almost forgot to tell—for several days in a row, I had noticed a hawk had been flying and circling over our orchard hoping to catch a mother hen off guard and grab one of her chicks. After a couple of days seeing it and taking off my bonnet and waving it at the hawk to frighten it away, I really got upset to think that he would keep coming back. I didn't know whether or not he had been successful in grabbing a chick, but I thought that I should do something. So I went into the house and grabbed Dad's old shotgun and, when the hawk made another pass, I fired. The recoil knocked me flat on my butt, and I didn't see if I hit the bird or not, but he quit checking us out every day.

The Geese

In 1930, when we moved back from Texas to the farm, Paw had been living alone all those years, but we found the farm to be surprisingly well equipped with all the machinery that was necessary to farm, and the house was well furnished. Mom said the feather beds and pillows had not been used for so long, the feathers smelled stale (or something). So she bought several geese and one gander.

That gander was as mean as a snake and chased me every time I was out in the yard unless it was midday and the gaggle was down in the orchard stuffing themselves. However, being a healthy, growing girl, I could run fast, and when the mean old gander came after me with his head thrust far out on his long neck with an open mouth that uttered a hissing sound, I could outrun him and hop up on the smokehouse porch.

Every now and then, this conceited animal would see Paw walking across the yard and take out after him. Paw would stop and turn toward the gander and wait until the fierce-looking bird got very close. Then Paw would give him a sharp kick in the chops, whereupon the deflated gander would turn tail and run. However, I did not choose to try it because my shoes were not the heavy plow-type shoes that Paw wore, so I just continued to keep a sharp lookout for this sneaky pest and bet on outrunning him.

Geese are strong birds. They can rise from a standing start and fly a great distance. Our geese would eat all day out in the field, then come up to the chicken yard about dusk and join the chickens when I fed them shelled corn. They were so fat that they probably could not fly off.

However, Mom did not take the chance. When we picked feathers each spring, she would take scissors and cut the end feathers off the tip of one wing to throw them off balance so they could not fly off.

Mom first got the geese when we moved back to Kentucky. We only had one gander and three or maybe four geese. Since they had the whole farm of about 165 acres to wander around on all day, Mom was concerned that they might tend to lay their eggs out somewhere and then set. So Mom told Paw and me that when we went to drive up the cows to be on the lookout for geese hanging out at certain places. If we told her that two or three days in a row, we saw them at a certain place, she and I would go down to check it out. Sure enough, an old goose would have about three eggs in a makeshift nest and be really hostile when we came up. Mom would scare the goose off while I grabbed the eggs, and we would take them back to the house, and the goose would have to start all over again.

A chicken hen could set on only about five goose eggs because they were so much larger than hen eggs, but Mom would do it, and when the little goslings hatched out they were the cutest little things you ever saw. You could put the baby geese in with a group of baby chicks and the mother hen would take care of all of them. In this way, Mom's flock of geese grew in number rather fast.

In the spring it was time to pick the geese as they would molt before summer anyway. So Mom and I would go out and catch a goose, and she would turn it upside down on her lap, holding its feet down under its tail with her left hand while she picked feathers with her right. You only pick the breast feathers and the down, which is thick and soft, and put it into a sack or a pillowcase. It doesn't hurt the goose. In fact, they seem glad to get rid of the heat.

Since the goose is belly up on Mom's lap, his long neck is tucked under her left arm, but that doesn't keep the head from wandering around nibbling at the flowers on her dress, etc. This would drive Mom wild as she was very ticklish. So she would have me hold the head of the goose while she plucked the feathers. When we tried to pick the gander, it was a different ball game because he would bite at me for holding his head. I don't know how long it went on that we didn't pick the gander, but someone told Mom to pull a man's sock over his head so he could breathe but not bite. This worked, and from then on we put a sock over all their heads and I picked, too.

One day, my sister, Betty, who was about four years old and small for her age, was out in the back yard and Ol' Gander slipped up behind her before she heard him and could run for the house. He was so close that, as she ran, she caught his head under her little arm. He tried to pull back to get his head loose, flapping his large, strong wings until she was just running in place and crying. I saw it happen and ran over as fast as I could, screaming for Mom to come help. Forgetting my fear of the goose, I started kicking him with all my might from behind. The goose started going forward as Betty ran. Then Mom arrived and picked up Betty while I kept kicking the goose—and enjoying it—until he ran off. By this time Mom had collected enough feathers to replace all the pillows and featherbeds in the house because the pickings were more fruitful since the gaggle had increased to about thirty geese. So she sold the geese and bought a start of turkeys, which I think were two females and one tom.

The Headless Turkey

Turkeys were not as aggressive as geese. While up in the chicken yard, the tom would display or strut his feathers in all his glory, but I don't remember being afraid of him.

The turkeys stayed down in the orchard most of the time and only came up to eat the chicken corn and to roost in the trees in and around the back yard. I don't know if Mom clipped one of their wings or not. At any rate, they could fly up in the peach and pear trees in and near the chicken yard. As the flock grew, so many turkeys roosting in the tree would kill it, and we lost several peach and pear trees to the turkeys.

Mom used the same technique to increase the flock, finding where they were nesting out and taking the eggs to put under setting hens. The turkeys would then get busy and lay another batch of eggs to set on. Anyway, the flock was getting larger and Mom started selling some to the peddler who came by our place each week. Money was scarce in those days, but the peddler came by weekly and would buy the eggs that Mom had gathered from the hens. Then she would use that money to buy coffee, tea, soda, baking powder and a few other things that we didn't produce. We used salt to cure and preserve pork in our smokehouse, so when we needed a one hundred pound bag of salt or a can of kerosene, Mom would call and ask the peddler to bring one to her on his wagon. Then she would sell him two or three frying size chickens or a turkey to pay for it.

One year, just before Thanksgiving, Mom said to me, "Everybody has turkey for Thanksgiving, so we will have one, too."

She read in a book that the way to kill a turkey was to tie a stout cord around its neck, then pull it up to a tree branch or clothesline, stick an ice pick in its throat, and while the blood spurted out, pick the feathers. Well, Mom said emphatically, "I can't do that!" Picture this shy little lady who thought nothing of taking a frying size chicken to the chopping block, whacking off its head, then pouring boiling water over it to pick and clean it. Well, we took the chosen turkey out to the chopping block and she promptly cut off its head. When she dropped it onto the wood chips, it did not stay there. The headless bird rose and flew out of the wood lot for about one hundred yards before coming down. Every animal on the farm was upset. The horses and cows in the pasture field bugged out their eyes, stuck up their heads, and ran off. All the chickens in the yard stuck up their heads making strange noises, and Popeye started barking and ran after the turkey. Mom and I stood there amazed, then Mom came to and shouted, "Run get it! Don't let the dog get it." I had to climb two fences to get into the field, but I was screaming at Popeye so he just stopped and looked at it with a puzzled look on his face.

Anyway, when we got it back to the smokehouse porch and poured boiling water over it, we frantically started picking its feathers. However, during its final flight, its body cooled off and the large feathers set, so we had to get pliers to pull out the wing feathers.

Everyone but Mom and I really enjoyed the Thanksgiving dinner.

Hog Killing Day

At the first cold snap in the weather, we would have a hog killing. If this cold snap came early or for some reason they thought it might not last, they would only kill one or maybe two hogs. Then when the weather really got cold, they would kill four or maybe five.

This being such a busy day, we would hurry and get our chores done, for everyone was assigned a special job to do. I was mostly their messenger. Mom would say, "Go tell your dad to send in more meat for the sausage." I would run out and tell him, and he would send in a big pan of meat. Then I would take over turning the sausage mill for Mom while she cut it in strips to feed into the mill. Then he would yell for me to go tell Mom to send out the fat trimmings for the lard pot. No wonder I grew such long legs because they had me running back and forth carrying stuff and delivering messages.

Sometimes we would have someone to come to help us during this time, usually someone who did not have any hogs because Dad would pay him off with lots of fresh ribs, backbone, sausage and a ham or two.

We hung some of the hams as well as some of the sausage in the smokehouse, but most of it was put in a large box and covered with salt. Mom always sewed up the sausage bags before that day. They were made of unbleached muslin about three inches in diameter and a couple of feet long. As the sausage mill ground up the meat, it came out of a pipe that the sausage bag fit on. Every now and then Mom would stop me from turning the mill, and she would squeeze the sausage down to the end of the bag so it would be nice and compact. Then she would tell me to grind more into it.

I really can't remember which came first, putting the hams, etc., in the salt, then hanging them over the smoke bucket or the other way round, but they called it "curing the ham." Paw would start a fire in a large bucket, then put in a layer of hickory chips. He would watch it closely, and if the chips would start to blaze, he would sprinkle it down with water so it would give the hams that hickory smoked flavor.

At every dinner meal, whether at noon or evening, we had potatoes, either boiled, mashed, fried or baked. We always had some kind of beans or peas, navy, lima, pinto or black-eyed peas.

However, when Mom fixed fresh pork she always cooked kraut, saying that fresh pork made one sick unless you ate kraut. I guess she was right because I never got sick eating fresh backbone, ribs, etc. She need not have worried, though, because I really like kraut the way she cooked it. I have always wondered if boiled cabbage was equally as healthy. Mom never said it was, but she cooked it regularly, and we all liked it as she always put in a large piece of pork and two or three pods of hot pepper.

Early in the spring, one of the first things we planted was a whole row of cabbage slips. She cooked some during the summer and made slaw, but in the fall they would take a knife like a machete and whack off the remaining cabbage heads and pile them up near the garden gate. Paw would cover them with straw or hay about a foot thick and cover that with dirt and a tarpaulin or something. When Mom wanted to cook cabbage or make slaw during the winter, she would pull the wad of straw from a hole in the side near the bottom and reach in and pull out a head of cabbage. Sometimes they stored turnips during the winter in the same kind of mound.

On the day of hog killing, one person (usually Paw) was in charge of the big iron wash pot or kettle. He would build a fire under the kettle and, after the dissection of the hog, the different cuts of meat would be passed to Paw. He would place it on the cutting table and trim off excess fat or scrap meat so the hams, loin, ribs etc., would have a nice shape. Then the trimmings would go into the lard pot or kettle to cook all the grease out. He would stir it with a large wooden paddle that looked very much like a boat paddle. Every now and then some of the meat would be lifted up on the paddle so Paw could see if it was done or not. He wanted all the grease cooked out of the meat but did not want to leave it cooking until it scorched, which would cause things cooked with the lard to taste bad.

When Paw said that the lard was ready, Dad or someone would help lift the cooked meat out with a large strainer that had a handle, putting the contents in a large bowl or pan. That was called cracklings. Some people thought cracklings were good snack food, but I never cared for them. Also, a lot of people liked crackling corn bread, but Mom would hardly ever fix it.

They then dipped the grease out of the pot and poured it through a clean cloth stretched over the top of a five gallon can to strain it and make more refined lard. Any trimmings that they didn't think were choice fat went into a pan to be cooked later, and that grease was strained and put into a different can for Mom to use when she made soap. The lean meat trimmings went into the kitchen and into the sausage mill.

Wash Day

When we first moved back to Kentucky, Mom did our laundry in the kitchen during the winter by heating the water to boil the clothes on the cook stove. The night before, I would pump and carry water to fill the washtub and two rinse tubs. We used a washboard equipped with a large bar of homemade lye soap to scrub the clothes. Then we'd hand wring out the soapy water and drop the piece into the pot of boiling water. The white clothes, sheets, pillowcases and tablecloths were washed first and, after getting boiled, they were rinsed in the clear water and dropped into the second rinse that had bluing in the water. All this plus the fact that they were hung on sunny clotheslines to dry kept the clothes looking really white.

Our better-wearing Sunday clothes were washed next but not boiled, but after the two rinses, they were starched and hung on a clothesline in the shade.

Play and work clothes came after that and, by the time the overalls were washed, the water was pretty cloudy.

During the summer, the tubs were filled under a large shade tree in our back yard, and the large iron kettle boiled the white stuff.

Money was tight during those years, so the only time Mom bought Lux flakes was to wash our silk hose. You could buy a large bar of PG laundry soap for five cents, but since we used a lot of soap, Mom made it. She would buy a couple of cans of lye from the peddler for five cents that would go in the grease from hog killing. I don't remember the formula, but after letting it "work" for a certain time, she added a box of borax. This was to keep the strong soap

45

from "eating up our hands." I don't know how many times a year she made soap because after making it and letting it set up and dry, she would cut it into large bars and fill a box we kept in the smokehouse.

Our New Washing Machine

All this work went on week after week until some time in 1935 when a truck drove up and delivered us a Sears and Roebuck washing machine. It was a beauty, having a nice large round tub with "balloon roller wringers." That is what they called the thicker, softer, rubber-covered rollers that were advertised "not to pull the buttons off clothes." Since we did not have electricity, we were pleased to see that it had a gasoline motor with a kick starter.

This new machine did not cut down on my work pumping water to fill the machine, the kettle for boiling whites, and the two rinse tubs. However, it was wonderful not to have to hand wring the clothes, especially the sheets. I never got the hang of coiling them around my left arm and moving up and over my shoulder the way Mom could.

This darling little jewel had an agitator that took spots off and cleaned grungy collars without wearing out your knuckles on a washboard. You did not have to jerk a rope until you were blue in the face to start the motor. It had a kick starter.

Not long after, even I could figure out why we got the washer. It became obvious that there would soon be lots of diapers to wash, and Mom must have spoken to Dad about it. I have to hand it to Dad for trying to lighten Mom's workload. I don't know what timeframe it happened, but Dad bought Mom a kerosene cook range that had four burners and a small oven. This saved Mom from having to light up the wood burning stove to heat water to wash the separator as well as do some light cooking or warming up food. Of course, he may have thought how it would save a lot of wood cutting and splitting as well.

Delivery of Ice

After Roosevelt gave us the gravel highway to town, a lady we called Mama Kitty, who owned an ice house in Bardwell, was asked by my dad and probably several other people along the highway to start a delivery route for ice. Although Dad had been picking up a large block of ice each Saturday, we had no icebox to keep it in so it lasted two or three days in the washtub. Later, she did start a delivery of twice a week, and we bought a large icebox and had them bring fifty pounds at each delivery. This helped Mom a lot because she could make Jell-O and other desserts, etc., on Saturday for Sunday dinner as well as tea for everyone.

It seems like Mom was always cooking a lot of food. For example, for breakfast she made two large pans of biscuits, a large platter of bacon, sausage, or fried tenderloin, two platters of fried eggs and sometimes scrambled eggs with squirrel or hog brains. We all ate like field hands, and I guess that is what we were, plus a whole lot more.

Mom's Family

Mom was the youngest of her family, and her sister, Aunt Muriel May Underwood, was eighteen years older, having been born April 23, 1882.

Their father, Wiley Marshall Underwood, was born February 29, 1854, in White County, Tennessee. He was raised on a farm on the Canny Fork River where the family owned and operated a gristmill. Their farmland was rocky and mostly hills but could be cultivated enough to grow a garden and grain for their animals. His father, Elijah, and all his brothers were carpenters. Although his father was a sympathizer for the South, he was

Wiley Marshall Underwood

deferred from joining the Confederate Army because he was the community builder of burial caskets and ran the mill to grind the cornmeal and flour for the community. We were told that after a battle was fought in that area he would drive his wagon to the site and pick up the dead, from both the North and South, and build caskets to bury them.

After the North won the war, the Yankee soldiers came and asked Elijah to swear allegiance to the North. When he refused, they confiscated his mill.

Aunt Muriel

Aunt Muriel Wilson About 1955

After this, most of the young Underwood men took their families and left White County, Tennessee. Some went to Texas and Arkansas, but W. Marshall and a couple of his brothers went to Kentucky. W. Marshall was a widower with two boys when he married Georganna Kirby, our grandmother.

Aunt Muriel was their first child and grew up to be a beautiful young woman. I was told that she taught school for a while before marrying Pat Wilson, a widower with two young boys. Therefore, she raised four boys of her own and two stepsons. I always thought Aunt Muriel was a remarkable lady and was told several stories about some of her activities.

She told me when she was a girl her family had joined a wagon train that was going to Texas for her dad to get work. Down in Texas they came to a small river that had no bridge, and wagon trains had been fording the river. There had been a hard rain and the river had risen above its banks, so they camped that night by the river. The next morning, the river had not gone down and the men were talking back and forth about whether to camp a day or two more or swim the horses and wagons across. About that time, a party of Indians rode up on their horses and, after talking with the travelers, offered to help get them across. Muriel's mother, Georganna, was terrified at this suggestion and didn't want anything to do with the Indians. This was because Indians had been rumored to steal children. Georganna's objections were eventually overridden because of the need. I do not know how old Aunt Muriel was at that time, but she said she had never been as scared as when she rode behind an Indian who swam his horse across the swollen river.

Aunt Muriel was skilled in many things, such as paddling a skiff without taking her oar out of the water so it never made a sound. She knew all about trees and could tell by looking at a board what kind of tree it came from. She was a good horsewoman, could hitch up and drive a buggy, and was one of the first in the community to drive a car. In fact, her daughter-in-law told me that she took Aunt Muriel to Cairo to get herself a new car when she was about seventy-five years old. The salesperson told her that a new kind of shift was on the new cars. They were automatic and made driving easy. Aunt Muriel told him that she didn't want any of that new stuff because it probably wouldn't last very long.

She told me another story about how all the ladies at church thought Aunt Muriel's hair always looked so nice. She and Mom both had naturally curly hair. So a lady told Aunt Muriel that when she died she wanted Aunt Muriel to fix her hair for her funeral.

In those days, Bardwell did not have a funeral home. So

when someone died, some of their friends would go over and prepare the body for burial, and one of the community men would drive his wagon to town and get the burial box and coffin. Some of the church men would dig the grave, and they used straps to lower the coffin into the grave. Young people in the community would offer to "set up" all night with the deceased. The community ladies would bring bouquets of roses or other fresh flowers to the funeral. Well, Aunt Muriel did such a good job on the lady's hair that she was called upon to fix the hair of most all the women who passed away in the community. On one occasion, the weather was very bad, and Aunt Muriel went to do the hair of the deceased. However, only one other lady showed up to prepare and dress the body. So the lady told her that she would just have to help her do it and, although Aunt Muriel said she almost balked at putting her hands on the dead woman, she did it.

When Aunt Muriel reached about seventy-five years old, her handwriting began to suffer. In fact, it got so bad that she bought herself a typewriter and learned to type. She loved it and started sending letters to the editor of our weekly paper as well as the Paducah and Louisville editors and even the governor. She scolded them for some of their editorials that she disagreed with as well, and she offered criticism or suggestions for projects for the good of the people in the county.

She was an avid watcher of the Lawrence Welk Show on television and kept up with all the regular performers. Once she typed a letter to Lawrence Welk, asking about Larry Hooper, a wonderful bass singer. She had noticed that for several weeks Larry had not been on the show, and she wanted to know what had happened to him. The next Sunday at church, she proudly showed her friends that Lawrence Welk had written an answer to her inquiry saying that Larry had had surgery but was doing fine and would be back on his program within a week or two. Aunt Muriel did not know that some typewriters had a type font that looked like good penmanship. Nor did her friends, and they, too, believed that he had written it himself.

On one occasion, the Kentucky Governor came to visit Carlisle County, and all the town's leading characters went to the courthouse to meet and talk with the governor. Our town weekly paper editor asked the governor if there was any special place that he would like to visit while in Carlisle County or any citizen that he would like to talk with. Whereupon, the governor said, "Yes, there is. I would like to meet and talk with Mrs. Muriel Wilson." Someone got on the phone and called Aunt Muriel and asked if she could come in to the courthouse as the governor would like to meet her. She drove right in, and when the governor asked her to tell him what was needed in her section of the county, she told him that the dirt road that came off Highway 123 and went by her house and all the way to Laketon was in terrible shape. She said it had not been graded for four years and that several culverts were out or in poor condition, and weeds and bushes had grown up until it was dangerous to pass another vehicle. In about three weeks, the Laketon Road was overrun with working men putting in new culverts and cutting bushes, while road graders, gravel trucks and other equipment kept the road hot running back and forth fixing it up.

Aunt Muriel was not a mean or bad talking woman. In fact, she was gentle and sweet talking even when she did not agree with an editor or someone. For example, she used tact rather than hurt a person's feelings when correcting them.

Uncle Henry Kirby, our grandmother's brother, was often a house guest for a few months at Uncle Pat and Aunt Muriel's house. None of the farmhouses had central heat but were heated by wood burning, cast iron, or heavy gauge steel stoves. On winter evenings after supper, the whole family would sit around the stove while reading, sewing, playing cards, etc., until bedtime, about 9 P.M. Uncle Henry was a sweet older man but had a bad habit of chewing tobacco while sitting around and talking after supper. No one objected to that, but quite often he would haul off and spit on the red hot stove. Of course, the heat would fry the tobacco juice and it would disappear, but Aunt Muriel could not stand it. So she called Tommy, her teenage son, into the back of the house and told him, "Tonight after dinner when we all gather around the stove, I want you to haul off and spit really big on the side of the stove." Tommy's eyes grew big with wonder because he did not chew or spit. Aunt Muriel put a loving hand on his arm and said, "When you spit, I am going to jump up and bawl you out good and proper for doing such a disgusting thing. Get it?" Then she smiled at him and he caught on. So they did, and I am here to report that Uncle Henry never spit on her stove again.

Paw's Family

Paw was descended from Yankees. They were the Gorhams from New Haven, Connecticut. A few of them were famous people in history. John Gorham married Desire Howland, the daughter of John Howland and Elizabeth Tilly who were passengers on the *Mayflower*. Nathaniel Gorham was a cousin who was a statesman, president of the Continental Congress, and signer of the Constitution. The owners of the Gorham silverware company are also distant cousins descended from Jabez Gorham in the late 1600s.

Sam C. Klutts,
Christine Ezell

However, as you can probably imagine, having such distinguished relatives couldn't continue forever, and sure enough it didn't.

Paw's father was James Judson Gorham who was born about 1826 in Savannah, Georgia. His parents traveled somewhat between New Haven and Savannah. My parents thought that it was likely that they worked for or with Eli Whitney. This is because Eli Whitney worked frequently in Savannah also and is buried in the same cemetery near them in New Haven.

James was a buggy trimmer. This meant that he made

Above: Paw's mother, Ellen Albright Gorham (right) with her daughter
Amelia Gorham Minter seated next to her, her husband Adolph "Dolph" Minter,
and their children, from left: Roy, Josie, Alma, Florence
About 1904

Below: Paw's sister, Elvira Jane Gorham Pamplin, seated, with her husband,
Wiley Pamplin. Standing, from left: Georgia Pamplin, Mack Pamplin, Irene
Pamplin, Omer Lee Pamplin, Beatrice Pamplin, Omah Pamplin, Jimmy Pamplin,
Howard Pamplin
1930s

Next page and above on this page:
Sawmill where Paw worked
1890s
Below:
Paddlewheel riverboat
1890s

the upholstery and put on the finishing touches to buggies. He came to Carroll County, Tennessee, shortly before 1860. It was said that he was no good and he, in fact, did not fight for either side during the Civil War. Then one day, around 1875 or so, he just disappeared, deserting his wife and several small children. Paw was always resentful toward his father after that. He has always been the black sheep in our family ever since. He did return to Bardwell, however, late in his life and in failing health. He stayed for a short time and then moved on. I don't think anyone knows what happened to him.

Paw, in his young life, was a timber grader. To do a job like this you had to be a whiz with your multiplication tables. It was his job to look at logs or trees and estimate the number of board feet of lumber that would be produced. This was critical in knowing how much to pay for the logs.

In the 1890s he worked, among other places, on a floating sawmill on the Mississippi River. He was able to get his wife, my grandmother, Ida Lena Klutts, a job on board the same sawmill as a cook. To this day I have an old photograph (shown at the top of page 57) of a woman standing on the second floor of a floating sawmill looking over the balcony railing. I feel sure this is my grandmother whom I never met because she died in 1904 when Dad was about thirteen.

Since Paw was now a widower and still working on the river, he was not able to raise Dad. Therefore, Dad was raised by my Uncle Jim and his wife with their

Paw's wife, Ida Lena Klutts
About 1893

children on their farm. Then, in the mid-1890s, Paw quit working as a timber grader and bought a farm near Uncle Byron and Uncle Jim.

Paw must have really loved Ida because he never remarried.

Sawmill where Paw worked
1890s

Back row, left to right: Parham Klutts and his wife, Mollie Klutts, Elisha M. Gorham, Ida Lena Klutts Gorham, Aunt Weed Gaskins, Rachel Gaskins, George Gaskins, Alice Bostick, E.M. Bostick

Front row: Maggie Klutts, Delmer Klutts, Albert Gorham, Sam C. Klutts, Ross Klutts, Christina Ezell Klutts, ??? Gaskins, ??? Gaskins, Charles Bostick, Lawrence Bostick

Como, Tennessee
About 1898

Saturday Night Baths

Let me relay to you an incident that could have changed the bathing habits of a lot of people back at the time when everyone took their Saturday night bath.

Kitchens were large in those days and, late on Saturday, the kitchen stove would be fired up to heat water for baths, so the kids and everyone would be squeaky clean for Sunday morning church. This did not apply to Dad because he had gotten a vehicle gas tank from a junk yard or somewhere and mounted it about six and a half feet up on the outside south wall of our chicken house. Daily, he filled the tank that held about fifteen to twenty gallons of water. The afternoon sun heated it sufficiently so that when he came in from the field and afternoon chores were finished, he could go out in the darkness or moonlight and take himself a nice shower before bedtime.

However, the rest of us in the family had to depend on water heated on the cook stove and poured in a number three washtub.

Daily baths required hot water from the teakettle, which was poured into a wash basin. We scrubbed ourselves with a washcloth and a bar of Lux soap. Although they were selling deodorant (Mum in a jar) in the 1930s, we were blessed by everyone having nose colds during fall and winter and, therefore, we could not smell anything. In fact, there was a magazine advertisement that said fifty thousand Frenchmen preferred "this" perfume. Obviously, the French didn't have hot running water bathtubs in their homes either.

This bath incident was written in the newspaper: A

maiden lady who lived alone was preparing for two of her friends to pick her up, and the three would be going to church. She got out the number three tub, poured in the hot water, and took her Sunday morning bath. After the nice bath, she prepared to get out and dry off but could not get out of the tub. She, being a fleshy lady, could not get out of the tub no matter how much she turned, twisted and tried. She was stuck.

At the appointed time, her friends drove up and sounded the car horn several times. When she did not appear, they went inside to see what had happened and found her crying and stuck in the tub. They both tried to pull her out but it did not work. So they decided that one of them would drive to the farmhouse nearby and bring the man back to help them. While waiting, for modesty's sake, the friend draped a sheet over the distraught maiden lady in the tub.

The man came, appraised the situation and said that a vacuum had built up in the tub that created a suction, causing her to be stuck. So he went out and got a hammer and nail. He turned the tub and lady over on their side and, after much pondering, decided on the strategic place to drive the nail. Then he did. There was a swish of air and the lady slid out on the floor.

Thereafter, I made a vow, never to get so "fleshy" that I could not bathe in a number three washtub.

The Watkins Man

Before Roosevelt had the highway built from Bardwell to Berkley and on to Columbus, a peddler who came along the road in a covered wagon every week serviced all the families along the route. He stocked a line of household staples so a housewife could buy a box of kitchen matches, coffee, baking powder, soda, etc., as well as tobacco and snuff. He also bought her chickens and eggs.

Then there was Sears and Roebuck and a few other mail order catalogs that enabled the housewife to order almost anything she needed. The mail carrier would bring it right to her door. Therefore, there was no need for her to make the uncomfortable trip into town.

We also had a salesman who came around in a buggy because he sold drugstore-type items. He was called the Watkins man, and we would stock up on carbolic salve (a small tin for the house and a very large tin to treat the animals), mentholatum, cough medicine, laxatives, Epsom salts, borax acid, aspirin, lye and camphor, to name a few.

Most of the farm families treated their stock and their family members and rarely went to a doctor or took their animals to a vet. In fact, Paw knew how to treat almost anything that got wrong with the animals.

For example, when clover came up in the spring, it must have tasted mighty good to the horses, for sometimes they would eat too much and become bloated. Once, when this happened, I saw Paw mix up Epson salts and pour it into a large bottle that had a long neck (a magnum bottle). He put a halter on the horse and threw the reins up over a rafter in the barn and pulled the horse's head upward. Then he put the neck of the bottle down into the horse's mouth, and the horse couldn't do anything but swallow the Epson salts. I guess that fixed the bloated condition because the horse didn't die and didn't even look sick.

A friend of mine told me of a cow on his farm that ate wet clover and became so bloated that they thought she would surely die. They called a vet, and a large, disheveled looking, cigar-smoking guy arrived with a six-foot flexible plastic hose. He proceeded to insert the hose into the cow's rectum and slowly push it into the cow while smoking and talking to the owners. After a few minutes, the hose suddenly entered a pocket of gas that was expelled with such force it was ignited by the cigar. The poor cow ran off looking like a rocket with a five-foot exhaust.

When any of our horses, cows or other farm animal got hurt by the barbed wire on a fence or something, Paw would pour alcohol on the wound, then smear a lot of carbolic salve over the place, and it always seemed to heal it.

The Watkins man always seemed to time his trip so as to arrive at our place a little before lunch. When our men were working in the field, Mom always fixed a good lunch. She would ring our large metal dinner bell about fifteen minutes before she started putting lunch on the table. When the bell started to ring, the mules knew that they could stop where they were and get unhitched from the plow or whatever and be taken to the barn to be fed and the wood lot to the water trough. Mom would always ask the Watkins man if he would like to stay for dinner, and he always said yes, he would like to. Paw and Dad always enjoyed having dinner with this man (I can't remember his name) as he covered our county and some of the other bordering counties and could fill them in on politics, other news, and gossip. The mules were glad to have this man come around as they got about an hour of extra noon rest. After eating, Paw and Dad always bought items that they were getting low on. Since he not only enjoyed a good meal but also sold a pretty large order and got his buggy horse fed and watered, it is no wonder that the J.R. Watkins man always managed to arrive at our house just a little before lunch each trip.

While it comes to mind, let me tell you more about our large, cast iron dinner bell. It not only served to call the field workers in to the house at lunchtime but it served as our warning/alert system. Anytime an emergency occurred at the house, or if an important visitor arrived, Mom would go out to the post where the bell was mounted and pull the chain (probably a certain number of times) whereupon Dad and Paw would stop work and rush to the house.

Hobos in our Barn

The new highway was celebrated as such a great thing that Roosevelt did for our county, but there was a dark side about it, too. We started having hobos traveling through on the highway. The highway split our farm in half and barely missed a corner of our barn. Thus our barn hayloft was a convenient place for these travelers to bed down for the night. I have no idea why they would be on our highway unless they had gotten off a freight train at Bardwell, and maybe they were going to Columbus to catch a ride or work on a river boat that tied up there.

Paw had gotten so he would take Popeye and make a check of our barn and hayloft at bedtime. He was concerned that if someone was bedding down there for the night they could smoke a cigarette or start a fire to cook something and possibly burn down our barn. When Paw would find someone in our barn, he would ask the stranger if he wanted something to eat and bring him up to the back porch. He would call Mom out and ask her to fix the hobo a lunch to carry with him. Mom always had enough on hand to give the man enough food for two or three good meals. Then Paw would walk the man back down to the highway and explain that he could not allow him to stay in the barn. So far as I know, Paw never had any trouble getting the traveler to move on.

One time Paw brought a man from our barn and it was just as we were getting ready to have our supper. The man looked different—he had clean clothes and was clean shaven—so Dad asked if he would like to come in and have supper with us. The man did and ate heartily while using good manners and talking well enough. Near the end of the meal, he looked toward the living room and said something about our piano. Dad must have been surprised and asked him if he played. He said that he did, after which Dad said, "Well, play us a tune." The man went to the piano, sat down and started pounding the keys with both hands. We were startled as he kept pounding from one end to the other and never made a sound remotely like a tune or exercise. All the while, he smiled and laughed in an odd way. I was so busy watching him that I didn't notice Dad and Paw giving each other a signal, but they both stood up and stepped over to his side. Then in a low voice Dad said, "Sir, it is now bedtime, and you will need to be on your way." So Paw, Dad and Popeye walked the man down to the highway and probably waited until he was well out of sight.

I don't remember any other travelers coming up to our back porch, so maybe Paw and Dad decided to change our policy of giving them food.

Since the Roosevelt administration had started many programs to help needy people, the people who had been riding the rails were soon able to get work through these programs, and we had fewer hobos.

Dad Teaching School

Speaking of riding the rails, that brings to my mind a story about Dad teaching school in Berkley. Dad was living with Uncle Jim while he was going to school because Paw was still working on the river. He went to school until he was able to pass the Kentucky teachers examination. Then he quit and started teaching. This was around 1909. I have been told that Dad was a very good teacher. One reason was that he was a good disciplinarian. Due to this fact, he was asked to come to Berkley and teach.

Berkley was not an incorporated town. You might say it was a village. It had a general store, a couple of churches, a school, a railroad depot and a post office.

It also had several big boys who did not do farm work, could not get a job during the Depression, and had nothing to do but chew tobacco and play baseball. They played baseball until they were really good at it and could beat most of the nearby teams. They also practiced their art of pitching by throwing rocks at any and all of the unfortunate men who rode the rails through Berkley. I do not know whether this killed anyone, but the underground network for hobos and black men had spread the word to bypass Berkley.

Since these young men had nothing to do all day, they went to school because they had not passed to high school and did not care. Therefore, they thought it funny to "run off" teachers. They had run off several woman teachers at Berkley by unruliness and even intimidation.

A favorite trick of theirs was done with a shotgun shell.

Almost all of the boys were good fishermen and hunters, so it was common for them to have a leftover .22 bullet or shotgun shell in their pocket. So during recess they would take a pocketknife and cut open the end of a shotgun shell to pour out all the shot. Then when recess was over, assuming it was cold and the pot-bellied stove was going, they would pass by it on the way to their seat and toss in the shotgun shell. Usually it would take a couple of minutes for the shell to go off. This would give just enough time for everyone to get into their seats and the teacher to start writing on the blackboard. This would startle everyone except, of course, the one who did it. The blast would raise up the heavy, cast iron lids on the stove about four or five inches.

This tactic was successful in running off several woman teachers in Berkley, but it didn't work with Dad. He actually was the schoolmaster in every sense of the word. He could maintain order and discipline despite the best efforts of some of the boys who were as big as he was. This was before the days of "social promotion" and it was common for people who didn't make the grade to stay in the same grade year after year until they either learned their lessons or dropped out.

Usually Dad could figure out who tossed the shotgun shell and the culprit would get the beating of his life. Dad mostly used his belt, but he also had a paddle for special problem cases.

When Dad went there to teach, he sized up the situation and figured out how to deal with it. He would give the class an assignment. While they were working at their desks, Dad would walk up and down the aisles looking at their work. I don't know if he warned them or not, but I remember hearing that he would come upon a big boy who was loafing and jerk off his belt and have the boy whipped before he could get out of his seat. Some of the big boys shaped up and the others quit.

I don't remember which train ran through Berkley, but it was a different line from those that ran through Bardwell. During the Depression, on most every train that came through Bardwell, you could see several men riding on top of the freight cars.

Chestnut Ridge School, where Dad was a teacher.
Dad is in the back row wearing a tie.
About 1914

Rustlers

Another thing that happened on the dark side of getting the highway was rustling. I had heard reports that some of the farmers who had barns near the highway had lost hogs and maybe cattle from their barn lots.

Mom always got up early and fixed a large breakfast so we could eat and be out in the field or out doing our chores before the sun came up. One such morning, I had gotten up and, since it had gotten rather cool, the kitchen door was closed. I opened the door and stepped out on the screened back porch to wash my face and hands before breakfast. As I started to dry my hands, I heard one of our mules in a long lope coming up the fenced lane that ran from the barn lot beside the garden and back yard around the orchard to the pasture.

I went into the kitchen and said, "I just heard old Jack run by down to the pasture."

Dad said that he didn't think I did because all the horses had been fastened in their stalls the night before.

I have always had a smart mouth, so I said, "I guess I know that a horse ran down the lane. I could not see it, but I know it was Jack." I then said that the Ol' Mare could open the latch on a stall door and maybe Jack had learned to do it, too.

Paw and Dad got up and opened the kitchen door and went out on the back porch to have a look. It was beginning to get daylight so one of them said, "It looks like all our horses are out in the barnyard." They forgot about breakfast and went down the lane to the barnyard, and I followed because I was not afraid of any of our horses.

Sure enough, there standing around in the lot was the Ol' Mare and the two bay mules. The two mules had hemp halters on and a rope was on the Ol' Mare. Dad and Paw became excited because they knew that someone had been in the act of taking our horses until they opened Jack's stall door. Jack (being our wild-acting mule) lunged past them and ran down the lane. The fact that I had just opened the kitchen door and the lamp light was visible soon after Jack started down the lane probably led the rustlers to believe they had been discovered, so they took off. They had dropped a rope like the one on the Ol' Mare's neck, in front of Jack's stall.

I guess it was a cattle truck that had been backed up to the highway bank outside our barn because there were dual tire tracks at a place where they could have just walked our horses out the barn front door right into the truck. Dad got our brace and bit and bored holes in the front sliding door and the hinged single door so he could run a large logger's chain through the holes and secure it with a padlock.

Paw was so good to all our animals that it was strange that the mule, Jack, turned out to be so wild and unruly. When we moved back to the farm, Dad started working the horses to the plow, disk, or a triple tree hook, which was used to drag logs up to the wood lot to be cut into stove wood. He had to "break" Jack to the harness. However, over the winter when he would not be harnessed to work, he would return to his wild state and therefore have to be broken again each spring. Paw explained that whenever a young animal was born on our farm, he would always handle it a lot so the baby animal was never afraid of him.

However, Jack had been born the summer that Paw came to visit us in Texas. Dad had gotten Paw a "token" job helping the cook on the tanker where Dad worked as clerk and radio operator. Paw got to sail from Port Arthur, Texas, around the Florida peninsula and up to New York. The trip took about two weeks, and he stayed another week or so before returning to Kentucky. Paw had really enjoyed the trip and, for the rest of his life, would refer to something he did while on that trip. By the time Paw got back to the farm, though, Jack was already a wild little colt.

All the farm animals liked me (with the exception of Jack) and when our pond dried up during a hot, dry summer, I pumped water for them into the large watering trough in our wood lot. As the cows were let out of the barn each morning, they would come up the lane to the wood lot so they could come to the trough and drink all they wanted before going to the pasture for the day. Then at night they were again let in to drink before going to the barn. The horses were next to drink but never while the cows were in the wood lot because the mules would tease the cows.

I pumped water for them all, which was a lot of pumping. So at times Paw would take over the pumping to give me a rest. I would then climb up on the wood lot fence and Buck or sometimes Kate would come over for me to pet them and scratch between their ears. Once I had been petting Buck and, when Kate came up, I started petting her. Buck got jealous and bit the calf of my leg with his lips to get my attention. You talk about pain! You haven't

Above: Dad's Corps of Engineers
towboat *Corregidor*
at Memphis
1950s

Below: The *Corregidor*
pushing barges on the Mississippi
1950s

been in pain unless you have been pinched by mule lips! After that, I always made sure that Buck got most of my petting.

One day I wanted to visit my cousin who lived about three miles away. The Ol' Mare had been loaned out to make the "third" on a triple tree, so I went down to the barn and saddled up Buck to ride. The horse saddle didn't fit on the mule's straight back, so I took it off and just rode him bareback. I spent the afternoon with my cousin climbing cherry trees, eating cherries, talking and laughing. I told her I needed to start home sooner than when I rode the Ol' Mare because the mule was not as inclined to rush home.

As I got close to our house, I noticed that the whole family was out on the bank of the road in front of our house. When I rode up and stopped, Mom seemed upset and said they were worried about me because Buck had never been ridden before. I had not been aware of it because he had not acted nervous when I got on him so I patted Buck on the shoulder and said they should have known that we were pals.

City Boys Want to Ride

During the Depression, Paw's sister and family from Chicago would come to Kentucky for a couple of weeks' vacation. Not that we were any vacation resort, but it gave Aunt Janie and Uncle Wiley Pamplin (see picture, page 56) a chance to visit Paw, Uncle Jim and Aunt Myria's families. Also, their son, who drove them down, got a cheap vacation with plenty of good food and fellowship.

Aunt Janie and her husband had two sets of twins and several single birth children. On one occasion, Aunt Janie's son, who drove them down to Kentucky, brought his two boys. One was a little older than I was and the other a bit younger.

It was a hot, dry summer and I was pumping water for the horses that had come up into the wood lot. Someone had closed the gate out into the lane, so all the horses had to stay in until they all finished drinking. The boys looked at the Ol' Mare and asked Paw if they could ride her. I became jealous because I considered the Ol' Mare my horse. Paw wasn't keen on the idea, but they kept on until he said, "Well, I guess so."

The boys then started an argument as to which one would "stir." I was burned up that these "green horns" would be riding my Ol' Mare. I need not have worried. The Ol' Mare must have sized up the situation, for she took about six steps and jumped over the wood lot gate as clean as a whistle and ran off down to the pasture. We were all in shock.

Paw asked the boys, "Do you still want that ride?"

They both shook their heads and said, "No!"

The Cistern

During the summer, especially a dry summer, we had farm families from miles around drive their wagons with several wooden barrels to pump water for their household supply. Most of the farmhouses had water cisterns for their complete water supply. A large hole (about ten or twelve feet in diameter) would have been dug by their back porch or kitchen door. The cistern would be about twenty feet deep and plastered with some kind of concrete plaster. It would be finished off with a brick and plaster neck that came out of the ground for about three or three and a half feet. A small shed or at least a couple of poles that held a cross member would be set over the cistern to attach a rope or chain pulley to enable the lady or children of the house to draw up a full bucket of water. Most people had a wooden cover with a small hinged door that was large enough for the water bucket to go through. At all times, this little door was closed after drawing water so birds or small animals could not fall into the cistern.

Once in a while, someone would relay their experience about a cat or squirrel that had fallen into the cistern and died. The family would then have to draw out all the water. This could be several hundred gallons. They would then lower a member of the family down to scrub the walls of the cistern to remove any trace of the dead animal. Also, during a dry summer when all their water was used up, they would use this opportunity to clean and scrub their cistern before hauling barrels of water to pour into it.

The reason the cistern was near the back door or porch was that they had gutters on that side of the house with a downspout that had a flexible connection to the gutter. The family would not put the spout into the cistern until they thought the rain had cleaned the dust and any other material off the roof. Then a family member would run out in the rain (unless their porch extended over the well) and move the downspout so the rainwater would go into the cistern. This was usually the job of the lady of the house because the men were either out in the field or at their barn doing chores during a rain shower.

On the other side of the house that did not have water runoff into the cistern most people had a water barrel or two to catch water they used for washing and watering chickens etc., to preserve their precious water in their cistern.

The farms that depended on cistern water for household use would have a large pond to water their animals. Some folks had a large pond in their barnyard and another large pond in their pasture field.

Every few years, we would have a long, dry summer, and it was really hard for the farmers to provide water for their animals when the ponds dried up. We have had people drive their cows down the road and into our wooded acreage where our spring always had water. The feet of a lot of cows going down to drink from the spring would push mud into the water source until it cut down the flow of water. So Dad put on his hip boots and went down and dug the spring out real deep and sunk a barrel that he had cut out the top and bottom, where only a foot or two stuck out of the ground. This kept the water clean as it came up in the barrel and flowed over the top and down the ditch where the animals came up to drink.

The Pump House

I don't know how many gallons of water a couple of thirsty horses can drink, but when a farmer would drive into our wood lot with his wagon full of barrels to be filled from our pump, he would always unhitch the team and lead them up to the horse trough to drink. He would then hitch them under the shade of the walnut tree until he pumped enough water to fill all his barrels. Then before hitching them to his wagon to drive home, he would bring them up to drink again. Most of the men would then pump and refill the trough, but a few would just leave, and then I would have to pump to refill the trough so our animals could drink. This did not set well with me, but Mom would not let me say anything about it. She would tell me that maybe he felt like he had done enough work for the day pumping and filling all those barrels.

Another thing that didn't seem fair to me was that Dad and Paw had to work hard to maintain the pump, and I don't remember any of those people ever offering to help when it was time to "draw the rods and replace the valves."

Our pump house was about eight by ten feet with a door that was left open all summer, but during the winter we kept the door closed. There was a wooden gutter-type trough to pump water into that ran through a small opening in the wall out to the large horse trough. There was some kind of a pivot arrangement as the trough passed out of the building to the horse trough. When you needed to pump into a bucket, you could easily push the trough aside and hang the bucket on the pump.

The slanted roof had a removable panel over the pump that had to be taken off in order to draw the rods out. Dad would climb on top of the pump house and straddle the open panel section, and Paw would stay on the ground by the pump with a large pipe wrench that we called a monkey wrench. Paw would remove the part of the pump that connected to the pump handle mechanism so he could pull up the rod. Thirty or forty feet of wooden rods were probably pretty heavy, but I don't know how they did it. They probably tied a small gauge rope to the end of the rod so Dad and Paw both could pull the rods up.

Anyway, Dad, from his position on top of the pump house, would hold the rod upright so as not to bend or break it while Paw would uncouple that length of rod from the others. Then they would pull up another and uncouple it until they all were out of the well. On the bottom of the last rod would be a cylinder with leather plungers. A "foot valve or check valve" would let in the water from the water table about forty feet down and hold it. Therefore, we never had to prime our pump.

Since money was tight, Dad made the leather plungers from a good piece of leather using Paw's perfectly honed pocketknife to cut them out. For a few days after installing the new leather cup plungers they fit tight and pumping was hard, but we had plenty of help getting them loosened up.

Persimmons and Goats

When Dad first got back into being an active farmer, he said our crops needed rotating. The same fields had been producing the same crops for too long.

There was a large pasture field that bordered the barn lot with a large gate that let cows or horses out from the barnyard right into the pasture. He said he needed to plow up that pasture and plant a corn crop there. However, when he got the turning plow with a triple tree hitch out into the pasture, he decided he would need to wait another year before putting his plan into effect. The long use as a pasture made the sod very thick and the ground hard, but what really caused the delay was there were so many persimmon bushes that had such strong root systems. The roots caused the large plow to frequently hang up and the three horses could not pull it out. Dad would have to back the team up, then pull the plow back out himself. Since this happened so often, Dad changed his mind about plowing up that field to plant corn. So during late fall and winter while he was neither putting in a crop or harvesting a crop, Dad took a saw, double bit ax, pickax, spade, can of kerosene and matches and cut down the bushes. He even tried to dig up the hateful root systems or burn them out, but the next spring, what do you know—the persimmon bushes came up again and maybe even more.

Although Dad was very determined to make that pasture into a crop of corn, he wasn't gaining on the scrub bushes at all. So he talked about the problem with several friends. Someone told him that he needed to get himself a herd of goats, for they would not only eat the bushes but also chew up the root systems. So Dad purchased a few goats and a billy.

The goat family really went to town eating up the persimmon bushes and everything else in the field, but they were active little creatures and started going over or under the fences and eating up other crops, too. The older nanny goat was the matriarch of the herd, and wherever she went, they all went. Dad cut a one-foot section of a small (about four inch) tree and trimmed the limbs off, leaving one three-inch stub near one end of the section, which made a hook. He bored a hole through the other end of the section so he could pass a wire through and wire it to a chain around the goat's neck. After that, the goats stayed in that pasture because each time the nanny goat tried to go under or jump over a fence, the hook caught on the fence and stopped her.

Paw watched and if the goats didn't come up to get water (and I think he fed them at times), he would go walk the fence lines. Usually he found the old nanny had caught her hook in a fence and couldn't get it out. Sometimes when I noticed the goats close to the fence, or if Paw had let them in the wood lot to drink from the water trough, I would get my left hand full of salt and put a little in my right hand and hold it out to them. They would come up and lick salt from my hand. They were so cute and their little tongues were as dainty as a kitten's tongue.

Goats are very prolific since their gestation period is five months, and the females had two babies at a time. Within a year, the five females turned the herd into twenty-one goats. I don't know how the word got around that we had goats for sale, but around July Fourth and some other celebrations, Dad sold young goats for barbecue.

One day the herd came to the water trough, but Ol' Nanny was not with them. After Paw walked the fence lines around the pasture and didn't find her, we thought she might have died. So Dad and Paw walked over the entire pasture, but no nanny. I don't know how many days they looked before they had to give up.

About three weeks later, Mom was out in the yard getting the wash kettle set up for washing when she saw an odd looking figure coming up the hill on the highway from Berkley. She walked over to get a better look and saw it was Ol' Nanny. I was not there, but Mom said the nanny was covered with dust, and she was a lot thinner, and her feet were sore and looked like she had walked a long way. We never found out where she had been, but wherever it was, she thought about us and went through a lot to come back.

Tudor, the Royal Cat

Of all the animals on our farm, a female cat called Tudor was my least favorite. I don't know who named her Tudor or why, unless it was because she acted like she was royalty. I don't know whether she slept at our barn or somewhere around the house. She never came up to be fed, so maybe she found plenty of mice down at the barn.

Our closest neighbor was at least three-quarters of a mile from us, and if they had a male cat, I never noticed it visiting us. However, Tudor always seemed to be able to find a male cat whenever she wanted one because about twice a year she would bring three or four kittens proudly up to our house. I don't know how old they were, but their eyes were wide open, and they were already skilled in "play fighting" with each other and could run and climb quickly. Thinking back, maybe the kittens' appetites were getting too demanding for her milk supply.

Tudor knew that we ran a cream separator and that, after saving out milk for drinking and cooking, we poured the remainder of the separated milk in a five-gallon bucket that we kept on the smokehouse porch to give to the hogs. She just wanted her lively young kittens to be able to "pig out" on the milk before the hogs got it. The kittens were really cute, but wild, and I had to work hard to get to touch them. Tudor would leave them at the house while she went out hunting, which was probably quite a job to keep them with enough to eat. The thing I disliked about Tudor was that when she brought up her "kill" for her babies, she would not have killed it. She would disable the young rabbit or field mouse and let her babies have it. Then she would stay back a little way, but close enough that she could make sure the rabbit or mouse could not get away. I hated her for doing it and could not watch.

Dad was always upset when he saw the kittens, for although he wanted a mouser around the barn, five or six cats hanging around the smokehouse were too many. Although no one ever told me what happened to them, I think Dad would give the kittens to a family down the road. No sooner did Dad get the cat population cut back to where it was suitable than Tudor would supply another crop of healthy kittens.

Finally, Dad had an inspiration. Our family was going to Paducah on a shopping trip. So Dad sacked up Tudor and put her in the trunk of the car. He thought that instead of getting rid of the kittens, he would get rid of the kitten factory. So on the outskirts of the city, he opened the sack and let her out. We lived five miles from Bardwell, and it was another twenty miles on to Paducah. Although it took about a month, Old Tudor came back, and Dad did not have the heart to do it again.

Kick the Can

When we lived in Texas, I went to a large school that had a teacher for low second and another teacher for high second. We had a music teacher and a penmanship teacher who came to our room for that period. During lunch and recess, there were playground teachers, and we played London Bridge is Falling Down and Ring around the Roses, etc., under their supervision.

However, the one-room school in Kentucky had one teacher for all grades, and during playtime the older and younger children all played the same games. Scrub Baseball, Wolf over the River, Annie Over, and Kick the Can were the games we played. Our favorite was Kick the Can—that is, if someone could furnish the can. None of our families bought food, whether in a can or otherwise, because all the families raised their own food. Since cans were fairly hard to come by, our teacher would oftentimes furnish us with a can.

A can wouldn't last very long, as it was put in a circle drawn in the dirt, and the person who was "it" would hide their eyes and count to one hundred by fives while everyone else hid. Then "it" would leave the circle and try finding everyone. Of course, the younger children were easier to find, and it wasn't hard to beat them back to the circle to call them out. Some of the older boys were hard to find, and even then, they could beat "it" back and kick the can a long way out of the circle. This would free all those who had been called out, and while "it" was running to retrieve the can and put it back in the circle, everyone could run and hide again.

Some of the boys were very proud that they could kick the can so hard it went a long way out and also collapse the can. However, we couldn't play that game again until someone could furnish another can.

Fighting with Boys

When school let out, about one-third of the students went north on the dirt road, another group went across a field to the west, and our group walked south on the road. Several mean boys would leave school in a run to a grove of trees and cut a switch and wait until our group of girls walked by. Thereupon, they would run out of the grove down the road bank and run past the girls and switch their legs as they went by. If they switched my leg, I would hit them with my lunch box. Within a few weeks after school started, the new lunch box Mom bought me for a quarter would be bent out of shape and the lid wouldn't close. That was it. Mom only bought one lunch box a year for me. After that I had to carry my lunch in a one-gallon sorghum bucket.

The oldest boy going our way was my age and grade, but I had grown taller than he was. So after getting whacked by my dinner bucket a lot, he quit switching my legs, but he would run by and switch the little girls' legs and get them crying. This upset me so much that the next time he made a pass, I would grab him and we would fight. I still have a few scars that resulted from those fights while going home from school, and my lunch boxes were always banged up from bashing boys in the head with them.

The Missing Glass Door Pane

I was fourteen when I passed out of the eighth grade at Chestnut Ridge County School, but when I started to high school, the county school bus came by and took us to Bardwell High School. This was the year 1935. I had a new little brother, Joe, born on July 14. Dad was very pleased because I was getting too "ladylike" to be the farm tomboy. Now he would have a real boy to take my place.

I don't remember what year it happened, but in 1936 or '37 the Chestnut Ridge School closed and all the children were sent to the Bardwell School by bus. Several children who lived beyond our house would stop in at our house and wait until we heard the bus shift gears coming up the Berkley hill. Then all the kids would grab their books, coats, lunch, etc., and beat it down to the highway to catch the bus.

One little girl, Marcella Phelps, who was the only child of her family would get to our house quite a bit early so she could play with our babies, Joe and Sue. Everyone enjoyed these morning get-togethers and often, in their haste, someone would jump up and run for the bus, forgetting something. So Mom would survey the room when they left and, if something was left, she would go to the door and yell, and that person would come back and grab it from Mom. The others would drag their feet a bit climbing on the bus to give that person time to make it back.

When fall winds and cooler weather started, we would start closing the front door to keep the house comfortable, as it was not cold enough to set up the heating stove. At that time, none of the country people locked their doors, even if we were gone all day to town or anyplace, the doors were left open.

At some time during the summer, one of the four large glass panes had been broken out and, since we didn't close the doors anyway, Dad had neglected taking the measurements to town to buy another glass. This went on for several weeks. As the kids ran out each morning, they slammed the door behind them. If Mom found something they had forgotten or dropped, she would run over and stick her head out through the large empty pane to call them to come back. In the early days, the schools did not have lunch service, so when someone forgot their lunch, they didn't eat.

Fall started turning into winter, and Dad "put up" our heater, but having that large pane out rather defeated the purpose of trying to heat the room. Therefore, that Saturday while he was in town, Dad got the glass and some putty and promptly installed it.

It all went lovely until Monday morning when someone yelled, "I hear the bus!" and they all jumped up and ran out, slamming the door behind them. Mom gave the room a quick once over and spotted a lunch that had been left behind. She then ran over and stuck her head through the glass pane where the hole used to be to call out, "Lunch, lunch." It is a thousand wonders that the flying glass didn't cut her up badly, and we were all thankful that it didn't. However, it just so happened that at the time the door glass broke, a man from down the road was walking past our house. This was a very nice elderly man, but he had been struck by lightning that caused a very noticeable "tic" and a slur in his speech as well as a startled look in his eyes.

Dad replaced the glass the next Saturday, but for years after, he would tell about the incident, saying that Mom stuck her head through the glass to see Clarence go by. I always thought this was so mean of Dad to tell it like that because Mom had always been a beautiful but shy lady and it embarrassed her to no end.

Eavesdropping on the Party Line

In 1930, when we first came back to our old Kentucky home, TVA was just a gleam in Roosevelt's eye, so we had no electric lights, iron, radio, etc. However, we did have a telephone. It was a wall-mounted phone that ran on two dry cell batteries. I don't know what the batteries did because we had to turn the crank to ring anyone.

There were about ten families on the line, and these families had to maintain the lines that went into Bardwell where the central office was. The men would all arrange to meet about twice a year and walk the line to cut away bushes or fix a broken insulator or anything that might hamper the service into "Central." They tried to schedule these meetings on an off season rather than planting or harvesting season. Of course, should we have had a storm or some accident that knocked down a pole, they would meet and take care of that. Since they owned and maintained the line, they paid about five dollars per year to hook up to Central.

The central office had a lady who ran the switchboard. I think it must have been in her house because she answered day or night when you turned the crank to make one long ring. Others along the line had different ring signals assigned to them. Ours was a long, a short, then another long. One of my school friends had a long, long, short ring.

While the men enjoyed the maintenance meetings, getting together and visiting with their neighbors, the wives would send food. Then the wives enjoyed the phone all the rest of the year. Everyone knew everyone on the line as well as their ring and would pick up the receiver and eavesdrop. If the housewife was busy, she would become more selective and only pick up when certain people received a call. However, when the ring was one long ring for Central, most all would pick up just to see who was calling out of our community.

Mom's sister, Aunt Muriel, was on another line and she had to call through Central, and you can bet everyone knew what she and Aunt Muriel talked about. I don't know if it was because Mom was shy and didn't want her conversation overheard, or because she was so busy, but she rarely talked or listened over the phone. Most of the women were not as busy as Mom, or maybe they had more kids to do their work, but some of them would stay on the phone daily for long conversations. In case you needed the phone and after trying a couple of times, you could interrupt them and ask if they would let you use the line for a short message. They were always nice about promptly hanging up to let you use it, but you can bet they eavesdropped to see what was so urgent.

Dad's Homemade Radio

We took the *Carlisle County News*, a weekly publication of about four pages. This told of marriage and death notices and other matters that happened at the county courthouse and not a lot more. Dad subscribed to the *Veteran's Magazine*, and Mom took a needlecraft magazine, and that was about it.

Aunt Muriel had three large boys who still lived at home, and they read a lot of five-cent pulp magazines. After they finished reading them, she would bundle up a bunch and bring them to me. I read so many of these cowboy stories that I knew how they would end by the time I was halfway through.

Our town of Bardwell did not sport a library, so at night we just sat around the wood burning heater and ate chestnuts, walnuts, etc.

Dad, having been a radio operator while working in Texas, decided that he would build us a radio. He rummaged around in his box of used parts and built a radio that supported three headsets, which he hooked up to an old car battery. It was wonderful. We could listen to *Amos and Andy*, *Lum and Abner*, and the *Nashville Barn Dance*.

Of course, me and my big mouth, I told all my friends about funny things I had heard Amos and Andy say over the radio. Soon everyone on our line knew we had a radio, and quite a few people would walk about a mile to come over and hear *Amos and Andy*, etc. We only had three headsets, so Dad would take one ear piece off the headset and then six people could sit in a ring around the radio and enjoy the program.

Dad built our radio probably in the late fall or winter of 1930. However, three or four years later, with the Depression easing up a bit, Dad ordered us a nice table model radio from Sears. This radio had a packaged replaceable battery and a loud speaker. By then, some other people in the neighborhood were also getting radios. The programming had improved, too. I loved to hear *Jack Armstrong, the All American Boy*, *The Shadow*, and the *Lux Theater*.

The Old Teakettle

While I was in school, I was told that Robert Fulton invented the steam engine resulting from many years of watching the steam escaping from his mother's teakettle on her kitchen stove. The steam also lifted the kettle lid somewhat when the fire was really hot. I really don't know who was the smart lad who did it: Robert Fulton in 1802, James Watt in 1763, or Thomas Savery in 1698. But they were all steam power wise.

Likewise, Mom depended on our cast iron teakettle for so much. Each evening as I pumped the household water to fill a row of buckets on the shelf on our screened back porch, I also filled the teakettle. Anytime one came into the kitchen, they were aware of the teakettle with hot steam coming out the spout. Care was taken by all not to get too close. The full kettle was so heavy, as well as hot, that Mom had to use a pad in both hands to lift it and pour.

I have already mentioned that Mom fired up the wood burning cast iron cook stove each morning to cook breakfast, for the noon meal, and again in the evening, and the cream separator had to be washed and scalding water poured over all its parts twice a day. Also, the three-gallon milk buckets had to be washed and scalded.

Outside of the items that our family bought from the J. R. Watkins man, we had no household disinfectant, mouthwash, insect spray or other pharmacy aerosol stuff that we take for granted today. The hand fly swatter controlled all flies that made it into our screened porch. DDT was not introduced into our part of the country until a little before World War II. Baking soda and a salt solution acted as mouthwash and treatment for other irritations such as bee stings. However, there was no great need for anything other than scalding water from the teakettle. After hand washing and rinsing the dishes, Mom would pour scalding water over them. When canning fruit, vegetables and some kinds of meat using Mason jars, she always scalded the jars, tops, and rubber sealing rings.

All our towels, bed sheets, bolster and pillowslips, underwear, etc., were made of white cotton material. After they were washed with lye soap on a washboard, they were thrown in the cast iron wash kettle and boiled. Therefore, as kids, we were normally healthy and rarely, if ever, passed from one to another colds or any type of contagious diseases.

Visiting with Mrs. Blackburn

I must tell you about my friend, Mrs. Blackburn.

Shortly after moving to our Kentucky farm, I became acquainted with the middle-aged or elderly lady who lived about a half mile down the road past our house. Her husband's name was Cal, but I can't remember ever seeing him. So maybe she was a widow who lived alone in the log house with a huge fireplace.

The living area was very large and it had an added on bedroom and kitchen with a small back porch. Everything was always spotlessly clean.

Although all my family knew her, they were not friends as she did not attend our church or visit us. She must not have had a phone because she was not on our party line.

I can't remember how I got to know her, but I loved to go down to visit her for a couple of hours in the afternoon. She always made a big "to do" about me visiting her and would give me some cake or pie or something to eat that I thought was wonderful. Although I was only about eight or nine years old, she talked to me like I was grown-up and treated me like I was important company.

We would go out into her garden and she would proudly show me her vegetables as well as rows of flowers—and not a weed in sight. The garden flowers were probably annual flowers, for she would then take me around in her yard and show and explain her plants to me.

I don't know how she did it, but she always seemed to know everything that was going on with all the families for miles around. So when she would ask me about something or someone, I would open up and tell her everything I knew or had heard. Actually, this was probably the reason Mom and Dad were careful never to discuss family matters or gossip in front of me.

In early spring, her irises and spirea would be blooming, and I would think they were so beautiful. She would say, "Darling, would you like a start of this?" Whereupon, she would take a small spade and dig up a clump, then explain how to plant and care for it.

Now, Mom did not work out in the garden much, but she loved roses and had a long row of beautiful roses in our front yard. Twice a year, when we cleaned out the henhouse, she would have me put the manure around her roses.

First, I came home with irises and hollyhocks and, within a couple of years, hollyhocks were all over the space between the front yard and the orchard. Although Dad never told me, he must have liked them because he didn't disk them up when he sowed oats in the orchard each spring.

Mrs. Blackburn also gave me starts of red and yellow chrysanthemums, verbena, and a lot of other plants. Some were not so hardy and did not survive. I planted small spirea plants around the front of the house and porch, and in later years, I thought they were so pretty when they bloomed in the spring.

When she gave me a start of asparagus, I was not prepared for the large, beautiful fern that it turned out to be. Mom used these asparagus fern stems to fill in around the rose bouquets that she sent for funerals, etc., as they did in those days.

One day, out of the blue, Mom said, "Clydeane, why

don't you take your little sister (Betty, age seven) down to visit with Mrs. Blackburn, and you can stay all afternoon." Mrs. Blackburn obviously had been expecting us because she really poured on the pie or cake while we talked. Then she brought us tea or lemonade. She sat and talked with us and showed us all her treasures and keepsakes. I had already seen them, but Betty had not.

After a while, she took us out into the garden, then around the yard, taking a lot of time to explain everything to Betty. She had never treated me like that, but then Betty was younger and quite a bit smaller for her age, and I guess Mrs. Blackburn thought she was a baby. So I went along with it.

A few hours later, a car drove up and it was Mom's sister, Aunt Muriel, who had come to get us. Aunt Muriel was all smiles and told us that a surprise was awaiting us at home. When we went into the house, there was Mom in bed with a new little brother named Joe. I was happy about it, and so was everybody except Betty. Betty felt that the little boy had come to take her place as the baby of the family.

I was just a little hurt that they hadn't tipped me off as to why we spent the day with Mrs. Blackburn. After all, I was almost fifteen years old.

New Sleeping Arrangements

Upon the arrival of our little brother, the sleeping arrangements had to be adjusted. Although Betty was seven years of age, she was rather small and was still sleeping in her crib. I was not too thrilled about it, but Betty was assigned to sleep in my bed, which was in our parlor. This room contained our davenport and two matching chairs, library table, piano, Dad's trunk, and my bed. The room was rather crowded and had no room for a heater, so during the winter it was very cold. I had so many quilts on my bed, I could hardly turn over.

Our large living room had a large bed as well as the large baby crib, the heating stove, lamp table, a dresser, a sewing machine, and a lot of chairs where we sat before bedtime.

Dad contacted Uncle Dolph Minter, Paw's brother-in-law (see page 56 for photo) who lived in Cairo, Illinois, who was a very good carpenter. He came and lived with us several weeks while converting our long back porch into two rooms. One was to be the new bedroom for Betty and me. The other was back by the kitchen. So they made it into our dining room. That left us with no back porch except the smokehouse porch, which was not screened but large enough to set up the new washing machine and the two rinse tubs.

I really liked the new bedroom. While it was rather small, it had double windows and was furnished with a double bed, my dome topped trunk, a dressing table with curtains that matched the window curtains, and a chest of drawers.

Ironing with Cast Iron

While going to high school in Bardwell, I had to fix my lunch and be ready to catch the school bus before daybreak, so my folks did not expect me to do any morning chores such as milking, etc. Mom started doing the wash on Friday, and that night we would sprinkle and roll all the starched garments so I could get an early start ironing them Saturday morning. Mom would be cooking breakfast, washing those dishes, washing and scalding the milk separator and milk buckets, and most of the time she would then cook a couple of pies or a cake for Sunday dinner.

She had to keep the stove hot because I ironed with "Sad Irons." The wonderful material called "wash and wear" had not been invented at that time, so the heavy flat irons had to steam out the wrinkles in all our clothes. Mom did not expect me to iron our bed sheets, since drying on the clothesline did not wrinkle them. However, she did starch the pillowcases, and they had to be ironed. I could get finished and be ready to go to town around noon.

After spending the afternoon in town, we had to get home in time to feed and water the animals and chickens and do other chores, such as pump water for the house, bring in stove wood for the cook stove as well as the heater in the fall and winter. I did not have to help Paw in milking the cows and feeding the stock unless Dad was tied up doing something else, but the chickens and other fowl had to be fed and watered and eggs gathered. Mom had several chores to do as well as fix supper and get my little brother and sister fed and ready for bed. Then I had to practice a little on the piano and study my lessons.

Mom was busy from before sunup until sundown. She would also sew most of our clothes, but I really don't know how she ever found the time. She never had a spare minute to listen to the radio or eavesdrop on the telephone.

Chopping Cotton on the Fourth of July

During the summer when school was out, I again had to help in the fields. One summer we had more than usual rainfall, so Dad said we could not go to the Fourth of July picnic at Veteran's Park because we were so far behind in chopping cotton. Veteran's Park was a state park that overlooked the Mississippi River at Columbus, Kentucky. This was the site of a big Civil War battle where the Confederates had stretched an anchor chain from a large ship across the Mississippi to block the river to Union gunboats.

In those days, everyone dressed in their Sunday best and went to the park on the Fourth to visit with friends, listen to a string band play and the politicians speak, but at daybreak on that Fourth, Dad, Paw and I were out in the field chopping cotton.

Paw was always so sweet to have my hoe sharpened really well, and he and I would hoe adjoining rows with my row on the right of his row. Although I was pretty strong for my age, as the day dragged on, I would get somewhat behind Dad and Paw. Dad would say that if I didn't run my mouth so much I could keep up, and he would move on ahead of Paw and me. I guess Paw liked to hear me talk because he would reach over and chop cotton on my row a little so I could skip and keep up with him.

The sun came up in all its glory and found us deep into the cotton field, chopping and sweating. We heard a car blowing its horn, and there, coming by in a cloud of dust, were my friends, hanging out the windows, waving and yelling for me to come on to the picnic. I jerked off my sunbonnet and waved it at them, smiling all the while until they were out of sight. Then, like Scarlett in Gone With the Wind, I vowed that when school started again, I would take a course in something that would enable me to make a living without hoeing cotton on the Fourth of July, and I did.

Becoming a Bookkeeper

In those days, women could marry, keep house and raise children, or they could borrow the money and attend college for a term and earn a certificate to teach for one school year. They would then need to spend their summer at college to earn a certificate to teach another year. My cousin did this, but it took her ten years to get her degree. It was nerve shattering because at any time a person with a degree could bump you out of your job.

At any rate, when I chose my classes for my second year in high school, I took typing and shorthand along with my required subjects in the hope I could become a secretary. My years at training my fingers to play the piano helped me to become an excellent typist. I was a natural at learning shorthand because it is written as it sounds. However, when it came to transcribing my wonderful shorthand notes, I didn't seem to be able to get beyond the sound principle and was slowed down by having to check the dictionary on all my spelling.

By lucky chance in my senior year, the state had given our school the opportunity to offer bookkeeping. Since I had done well in algebra and geometry, I signed on for bookkeeping, although I had no idea what to expect. Our principal, Jack Gardner, taught the class, and I loved it and did well.

A Lucky Break—Going to College

After graduation in the summer of 1940, it was back to milking cows, feeding the animals and doing anything that needed to be done: pumping water, hoeing the garden or cotton, planting and picking tomatoes for the canning factory, and you name it.

About that time, the government had funded the NYA to give young people work for fifteen days a month at one dollar a day. Mr. Graves, our county school superintendent, had been given a position for one such youth to work in his office. He called the school and asked them to suggest a student who could type and do other office duties. The school recommended me.

I'll have to hand it to Dad because he encouraged me to do it, even though it meant that I could not spend as much time working around the farm.

I took the family car and drove into town about three days a week or so to work the fifteen days. Mr. Graves was very pleased with my energy at doing his typing, cleaning out, and catching up on filing, etc.

After working there a couple of weeks, I noticed that the bookkeeping desk was not being worked on. In fact, it was several months behind. I told Mr. Graves that I could add and balance all the journal pages because I had studied bookkeeping. He gave me the go ahead, and by the time I had all the pages balanced, I had figured out how to do the other part, even though it was single entry rather than double entry bookkeeping.

Mr. Graves was delighted because the person who had been doing the books had quit in a huff, and he thought that he would be unable to get a replacement. This went on through the summer and about a month after school restarted.

One Friday, Mr. Graves received a phone call from Murray College, telling him that the government program allowing two full scholarships from our county had not been used. Although school had already started, if he had a couple of qualified students, they would be able to take catch-up classes and not cost them anything.

Mr. Graves told the person, "I can't send you two students, but I have one who will be there in the morning at 8 A.M."

He hung up the receiver and said, "Clydeane, go home and get your stuff packed. You are going to college."

I respected Mr. Graves so much that I did not question his statement. I just picked up my stuff and drove home. Since it was Friday, Mom was out in the yard running our washing machine, and when she saw me turn into the yard, she thought something had gone wrong and ran out to meet me. I had worked up an excitement, so I said, "Mom, let's pack. I am going to college."

"When?" Mom asked.

I told her that I needed to be at Murray, Kentucky, which was sixty miles from home, at eight the next morning.

Again, Mom was quite calm and said, "Don't you think you should go down where your Dad is plowing and tell him?"

So I did, and Dad did not question the plan because if Mr. Graves, whom he respected, said for me to do it, I should.

Meanwhile, Mr. Graves had called a young lady who

108

had gone to Murray on this kind of program and asked her to call me and tell me what I should pack, etc. She called and told me to take the minimum of two sheets and pillowcases, two towels, a blanket, and an alarm clock. Luckily, Mom had washed that day, so we stayed up almost all night ironing my clothes and packing.

Well before 8 A.M. that Saturday, we rolled up to the administration office of Murray State College. They told me that I would be expected to work four hours a day in exchange for my tuition, room, meals, books and fees, which were about thirty dollars a month. Getting all this for only four hours' work was unbelievable for a girl who had been accustomed to working from before sunup to after sundown.

They assigned me to work in the office of the head of the Home Economics Department. Since it took me about an hour to do all her typing and other office work, I went about cleaning her stove and refrigerator, then changing the shelf paper and washing all the dishes on the shelves. She was so delighted with her sparkling kitchen that she bragged about me when having lunch with other department heads. This was a mistake for her, because the head of the boys' NYA Department had me transferred to work at the residential NYA Boys Building. It was okay with me to be the only employee to work in their office, type and keep their records, answer their phone, etc. I was able to do this and my class homework while there, which freed me up from having to go to study hall or the library each evening. Therefore, at my roommate's insistence, I tried out and became a member of the dance line for the annual Campus Lights show.

A Chorus Line Dancer

Most of the young people in this show were music majors who had high hopes to work on Broadway or somewhere else in the entertainment business. It was a good thing that I could do my homework while working on my job because each evening after dinner, we had to report to dance practice. While I was a farm girl, good at riding horses and other strenuous work, none of that prepared my muscles for the workout I endured during dance practice. However, all this was new and exciting for me, and the attention I received from the other cast members made all the hard work and sore muscles worthwhile.

Finding out that I had learned to do the steps and perform in our Campus Lights annual show well enough to make the cut for the chorus line gave me a feeling of pride and confidence. Since I had nice legs, could dance a bit, and could kick higher than my head, I did well in my role as a chorus girl. There must have been some talent scouts in the audience the night of the show because afterward I was offered a job in a chorus line in New York City.

Right here, I was faced with a decision whether to follow the personal excitement of being an attractive performer and deal with the attention of attracted guys, or to return to the world of using your brain to earn a living. I really never thought of myself as having an exceptional brain, but I opted to go with the "brain drain."

It is a good thing I made that decision because Mom and Dad would have disowned me for doing such a "shocking and disgraceful thing." They were so religious and prudish that no one in my family was even allowed to walk on the same side of the street as a beer joint or pool hall. I don't know if Mom and Dad ever knew about me "showing my legs" in the show, but I knew better than to ever tell them.

Left:
Betty and me
1943

Below, from left:
Joe, Betty,
myself, and Sue

The Attack on Pearl Harbor

On Sunday afternoons, after church at Murray, lots of us students would congregate in the student center on campus. Quite a few students were music majors, and there was always a lot of activity and music going on with a lot of laughing and cutting up.

On this one particular Sunday afternoon in December, I arrived in the student center to a totally different atmosphere. There was no music, no laughter, and no loud conversations. People were gathered in small groups, and the conversations were very quiet and subdued, almost like being at a funeral. I asked a girl near to me, "What is wrong?" She answered that the Japanese had bombed Pearl Harbor. I asked, "What's Pearl Harbor?" I had never heard of it.

She then said, "We are at war."

The next day, the United States declared war on Japan, and three days later, Germany declared war on us. Then, three days after that, classes were dismissed for the Christmas holidays.

In January, I returned to Murray for the next semester, but I really shouldn't have bothered. Things weren't the same. I had expected that several of the boys wouldn't return because they would have joined the service, but in fact, very few of the boys returned, and those who did wouldn't be there very long. Also, the entire atmosphere had changed. The war was not going well for America. Almost every day the papers were full of some new disaster for us. I began asking myself, "What am I doing here while such terrible things are taking place?" This was not a time to be sitting in class while such earth-shattering events were happening.

It is odd to think that an attack on a place that I had never heard of, such as Pearl Harbor, could have such life-changing effects on me as well as so many millions of other people, but it put an end to my college career.

It also did a lot of other things. It put an instant end to the Great Depression. It had awakened the economy, and American industry was coming back now with a vengeance. Workers and factories that had been idle for the last many years were now busy again. Because so many men had joined the service, jobs were now abundant, especially for women. In a country that was becoming increasingly devoid of men, women were now being asked to come forward and shoulder more of the load of keeping the home front going while the men were away at war. Therefore, I decided to quit college and join the workforce.

I had applied myself in school taking the type of business courses that would enable me to work in the business world. Therefore, I shouldn't have any trouble finding a good job, and I was determined that I would not be giving it up when the war ended.

It was amazing that in a couple of short years events had happened to totally change my life. I had been a barefoot girl working and playing on the farm in the depths of the Depression. I grew up and moved away to college, which put an end to that phase of my life. Then the attack on Pearl Harbor plunged us into war and ended the Depression. In doing so, it opened the door for an entirely new phase of my life, that of a working woman. So I guess you could say that in two years I went through a kind of metamorphosis from a barefoot tomboy of a farm girl to a young business woman in search of a career.

Left to right:
Sue, my dad, Betty, my son Robert Wall,
Joe, and my mom
1955

Above:
The Gorham children
on Sue's wedding day.
Left to right:
Sue, Betty, Joe, me
1960

Right:
Mom and Dad
1955

116

Epilogue

The date now is September 23, 2007. In three months I will be eighty-six years old. I have just reread this story again, and I am sitting here reminiscing about my childhood days on the farm during the Great Depression.

I have lived to see a lot in my time. I have seen the horse and buggy days, and I have seen men walk on the moon. I have seen wall-mounted, hand-cranked telephones and battery operated cell phones. I have seen the end of the Great Depression, the fall of Nazi Germany, and the collapse of the Soviet Union.

However, it was my childhood days I remember most fondly. In looking back on it, I think I had probably the best childhood that is possible for anyone to have. I lived in a veritable Garden of Eden. Everything was so healthy and wholesome for a child. I had a very stable home life and was loved by two hard-working parents as well as lots of animals. In fact, my best friends were animals.

By living on a farm, you learn the facts of life and also death firsthand because you witness it all. You learn what it is like to have to work very hard and for little or no money. You learn what it is like to have to do all jobs and not just the ones you like or the easy ones. Someone has to do it, even the dirty and disgusting jobs. You learn that work quite often requires you to get sweaty and dirty. You learn respect for all types of work and not to consider any type of work to be beneath your level of dignity. Along with this comes the respect for the other people who do these jobs.

You learn a healthy respect for all things—people first,

then animals, then things and property. You learn to love, care for and respect all types of animals, but by the same token, you learn that at times it is necessary to kill them for food. The Bible teaches us to have dominion over all the animals of the Earth. People raised on a farm don't have a problem with this. Although it was never discussed, we divided the animals into two categories: the animals that helped us work the farm and those that were raised for food. The animals that helped us work the farm, such as dogs and horses, were loved almost like members of our family and were very much our friends. It was necessary, though, that we not form emotional attachments to the other animals because we knew at some point we would need to kill them for food, although in my case it was difficult not to love baby goats. They were so cute.

Another thing was hearing about how so many people suffered during the Great Depression. We never suffered, or if we did, I never knew it. We always had plenty to eat because we raised it ourselves. We were never bored because we had so much work to do. We developed lots of different skills because we had to do everything for ourselves so we became very self-reliant, and self-confidence followed. We never had much money but we found that we didn't need much. This is quite different from our society now, which worships money. I am here to tell you that money makes a poor god. Just look at all those rock stars and movie stars and the self-imposed tragedies they suffer as a result of having too much money. Money is not so important to people who have had the experience of living without it.

I wouldn't trade my childhood experiences for anything

because I know I am a better person now because of that experience. The generation of Americans that survived the Great Depression and World War II has been called Our Greatest Generation. This is probably because of how we were raised. Hard work, discipline, sacrifice, and the experiences of those years produced a generation of confident and competent citizens. Most people seemed to feel that our problems were only temporary and better times were ahead. Even though conditions were quite often adverse, self-pity and self-doubt were not emotions easily found.

Questions such as "Can we survive this Depression?" or "Can we defeat Hitler?" were never asked because the answer was only too obvious:

"Of course we can because we are Americans."